ULU TIRAM

A cameo of life in Malaya at the time of "The Emergency"

by Peter Thomas
&
Kathleen Thomas

Brian,
Remembering our years together in 1st Bn and 1st,
Tommy

Leonie Press

An imprint of
ANNE LOADER
PUBLICATIONS

This book was written for our family and friends, fellow members of the Security Forces, planters and anyone else interested in Malaya at the time of "The Emergency." It is intended to be but a cameo of life there at that time as we saw it.

Kathleen and Peter Thomas

ISBN
1 901253 05 8
Published September 1997

Edited, typeset and published by:
Léonie Press
an imprint of
Anne Loader Publications
13 Vale Road
Hartford
Northwich
Cheshire CW8 1PL

Printed by:
Anne Loader Publications

CONTENTS

The author, who served in Malaya from 1948-62 with The 1st, 2nd and 6th Bns of The Royal Malay Regt. in addition to The Royal Artillery and a period planting rubber.

PRELUDE — 1952

She lay at his feet, still, silent, no longer writhing in agony. His carbine in his hands, he looked down at the young Chinese woman. She must have been in her early twenties — much the same age as himself — and he had killed both her and her unborn child.

It was of little comfort to him that he had ended her agony. The only thoughts going through his mind were that he was on active service in the fight against Communism and had been called upon to make a decision that would haunt him for the rest of his life. He felt sickened.

He became aware of the watching faces of his men as Corporal Hamid moved towards him.

"*Tuan...*" he made as though to speak, but Geoff interrupted him.

"Search her, photograph her and then bury her."

The order was given tersely and immediately put into effect.

The day had been uneventful until mid-day when the platoon found themselves on the edge of a jungle clearing where tapioca was being cultivated. On the North side of the clearing there was an *atap*-built hut which appeared to be unoccupied, and having observed it carefully for some time Geoff signalled to Cpl Hamid and two men to follow him. Then, weapons at the ready, they stormed into the building. As they did so all hell let loose.

Three Communist Terrorists (CTs), who had been hiding and watching their approach, opened fire on Geoff and his Corporal. In the ensuing melée a fearful scream had been heard as one CT fell mortally wounded and two others fled through the hail of gunfire for the jungle cover.

At Geoff's command the firing ceased and he and Corporal Hamid emerged from the hut mercifully unscathed. The other members of the platoon broke cover and a second CT was found lying in a pool of blood on the ground. A section of men was immediately dispatched to pick up the trail of the third one.

Corporal Hamid moved to check the body of the CT lying on the ground. As he turned the body over it gave a loud groan.

"Dia perempuan, Tuan, dia belum mati."

At his words Geoff moved over to the body. It was a woman, barely alive, her eyelids twitching as though she was conscious. That she was in great pain was obvious, also she was heavily pregnant, her swollen abdomen had been penetrated by bullets and blood was pouring from her. He looked at her face — the features were not those of a 'coolie', there was a refinement that not even the grimace of pain nor the drab uniform could hide. Slightly built with a mass of black hair which had escaped from under her red starred cap she had delicately arched eyebrows and high cheekbones. What must have been a beautiful face was contorted with pain and the pallor of death upon it called out for release. Her hand moved towards her mutilated abdomen and despair was both on her face and in her agonised whimper.

Geoff knew what he had to do. There was no hope of saving her, they were fifteen miles or more from any road and she would not survive the day. Any attempt to move her could only increase her agony. What he was about to do was totally abhorrent to him but there was no other way.

The men stood silently aware of the burden of responsibility that rested solely with their young officer. Geoff took careful aim: one bullet entered above her ear and she died instantly.

Wuh Pun saw it all from his well-concealed hole. One bullet from that bastard Englishman's gun had taken away everything that was dear to him. He watched the soldiers taking Ah Loy's finger prints, watched them bury her with their unborn child. He watched as the platoon silently moved off having similarly dealt with the body of his bodyguard Lim Meng who was killed in the hut.

The light had almost gone and the sounds of the jungle dusk came as a lament as Wuh Pun made his way to the grave of his love Ah Loy and the unborn child he was never to see.

He remembered the day that she had told him that she was pregnant, how concerned he had been for her safety and how she had dismissed his fears — refusing to go and stay in a safe place, repeating what she had said so many times:

"Wherever you are, I will be there also."

Four years previously she had said these same words when she had insisted on accompanying him into the jungle.

They had both attended the Clifford English School in Kuala Lipis. Four years her senior, he had left to attend the Nanyang University in Singapore where he had secretly become a Communist and dedicated his life to establishing a Chinese communist controlled Malaya.

On his return to Kuala Lipis on his third year vacation he had resumed his friendship with Ah Loy but they were no longer children and he realised that he was in love with her. Yet there was no time in his life for love — he was totally committed to Communism and would resort to whatever means were necessary to bring about its aims.

Ah Loy's father was a prosperous businessman. His interests were many and he was a respected member of the community. Wuh Pun's background was somewhat different, for his father was a contractor supplying Chinese labourers to the rubber estates.

It had sickened Wuh Pun to see his father go to great lengths to win the patronage of European estate managers. Socially they barely tolerated him but were nonetheless quite happy to accept cases of whisky and gin and other gifts at Christmas time. Likewise the lavish hospitality extended to these managers at Chinese New Year, with the air of assumed cordiality, had no impact on Wuh Pun. He was expected to be present on these occasions by his father. He used the opportunity to gather as much information as possible about the security measures in effect on the various rubber estates involved.

Wuh Pun's loyalty and efforts on behalf of the party were soon rewarded and he was appointed Political Commissar for West Pahang.

When Ah Loy heard the news she was determined to go into the jungle with him. To Wuh Pun this was unthinkable. No one other than she knew that he was a Communist. Her parents regarded him as unworthy of their daughter and he believed that the only way that he could marry her would be when Communism triumphed. Then his efforts would be rewarded and Ah Loy would be marrying someone of consequence — a Senior Member of the Party. She however, had been adamant that she should go with him and so it came to pass that she left her family and home. There were no farewells, just a simple note, which read: "I have to do this."

For one who had led such a sheltered almost pampered life she adapted quickly. She could shoot as well as any, studied Communism diligently and never questioned the means by which their campaign of terror and extortion was conducted. She became his most dedicated pupil.

The darkness was almost total, and he could barely distinguish the mound of earth on the two graves. It was time to go, there was much to be done, and his resolve was strengthened by his loss.

From the jungle canopy above a bird emitted a weird but strangely poignant call: *"Gelap tidor, gelap tidor, gelap tidor!"*

It was as though it called to Ah Loy: "Darkness is here, sleep, sleep."

Some five days later, at a makeshift altar, in a bizarre and most solemn ritual before three witnesses, Wuh Pun had his fingers pricked, he drank the blood of a freshly slaughtered cockerel and in a voice full of hate swore: ***to kill the bastard Englishman.***

CHAPTER 1

Geoffrey Farrer looked out at the familiar scenery, the *padi* fields, the most gorgeous pale green young *padi* where Malays, with their *sarongs* tucked up, were wading in the *sawah* — the wet *padi* fields. He saw the Malay houses on stilts in little villages of palm-thatched roofs built where clumps of bananas, *bunga rayas*[1] and coconut palms grew, with the mountain covered in jungle in the background. He was back in the country he had grown to love and was impatient for the long train journey from Singapore to end.

It was less than a year since he had left Malaya to return to UK and the poignant memory of the battalion's farewell was still fresh in his mind. He thought nostalgically of the three years in which he had been seconded to The Malay Regiment, a peak period in the campaign against the Communist Terrorists, who so nearly succeeded in taking control of that country as they did in other places. The trust and team spirit developed over these years was to form lasting friendships between all who took part.

It was not as a soldier that he returned, for he had embarked on another career. He had accepted the offer of the post of assistant estate manager, from one of the larger rubber companies, and was looking forward to the new venture rebuilding that ravaged industry.

He glanced at Sarah sitting opposite him and thought how young she looked, would she adjust to the change? She had certainly enjoyed the voyage out and their stay in Singapore. It had been a whole new experience for her and Geoff also felt that as he saw things through her eyes, he was seeing them for the first time.

1 *Malaya's national flower, the Hibiscus*

Sarah, watching the unfamiliar landscape unfold before her, felt hot and tired. She longed for a shower and a change of clothing. She wondered how long it would take to acclimatise to the heat and humidity. People obviously did, for not everyone looked as hot and sticky as she felt.

She glanced at Geoff — he appeared to be deep in thought, his eyes fixed on the mountains and jungle in the distance. Since leaving Singapore he had been slightly withdrawn and she had felt excluded from whatever it was that occupied his thoughts. She was probably being ridiculous after nearly four weeks of his undivided attention during the voyage on board *The Oranje,* which was also their honeymoon, not to mention the three days in Singapore, three fantastic days and nights! The time had now come to face up to the new responsibilities ahead. For Sarah it had all been a totally new experience, the visits ashore at Port Said, Suez, Aden and Colombo and especially the haggling with the "bum" boats in the Canal, added to shipboard life, had whetted her appetite for the life in the East.

She would never forget her first sight of Singapore and its approaches. The many islands, the Chinese junks, their coloured sails flapping gently in the warm breeze and the smaller fishing boats with outboard motors disturbing the tranquillity and calm. This was the Orient that up to now she had only dreamed of.

Many of the passengers were seeing all this for the first time whilst others gazed on what was for them a familiar scene, their faces displaying a variety of emotions. During the voyage they had met up with a number of planters and colonial officials. Some of these planters returning from leave in UK had previously been prisoners of the Japanese during what was referred to as "the Occupation." The harrowing experiences that they had suffered were perhaps brought to mind as they approached the "Lion City." Amongst the younger men about to become planters or enter one of the trading companies, a number had seen something of Singapore during their National Service, but for the majority this was their first glimpse of the Far East.

On docking at Singapore's Keppel Harbour they were surprised not to have been met by a representative of the company. Geoff was not perturbed. He knew his way around so they took a taxi to The Adelphi Hotel in Coleman Street and booked in, telephoning the Ulu Tiram Estate in Kajang that night without success. Meantime Singapore was there waiting to be shown to Sarah. The following day was Sunday and a further attempt to phone the estate met with no response. They booked seats on the train for Monday morning and sent a telegram advising their estimated time of arrival at Kajang Station.

CHAPTER II

The train was now approaching Kajang Station and they collected their hand luggage together.

"I will jump out as soon as the train stops and go and unload our baggage from the guard's van," said Geoff. "You wait here."

He jumped down onto the platform as the train stopped, leaving Sarah in the air-conditioned buffet car with the hand luggage. Quickly he moved to the rear of the train to unload the heavy stuff.

The platform was packed: Malays, Indians and Chinese were either getting on or off the train or meeting families and friends. Sarah was watching her husband move down the line of the train when she saw him stop and approach a large bad-tempered looking European man accompanied by a Malay wearing a khaki uniform and black *songkok.* Geoff shook the big man's hand and Sarah came to the conclusion that this was the estate manager Henry King, *Tuan Besar* of Ulu Tiram Estate. What she did not realise was that he had in fact met the train for the past two days!

Geoff having introduced himself quickly moved to the guard's van and unloaded two wooden cases and three suit-cases. Just then there was a shrill whistle blast and the train slowly moved off, next stop Kuala Lumpur.

"Shit!"

Geoff dived onto the train leaving Henry King open-mouthed as he watched his new assistant manager disappear and for all he knew go off to Kuala Lumpur for a few days!

Sarah's unease turned to panic when the train moved off but almost immediately Geoff burst back into the buffet car, shouting to the conductor, a little Indian man in a smart uniform: "Stop the train!"

Subramaniam, third generation of railway conductors, looked amazed.

"Simply, it is not possible, Sir."

"Stop the train, man, or I will," thundered Geoff.

Geoff already had his hand on the communication cord when Subramaniam leant out of the window, blowing his whistle and waving his red flag. The train shuddered and came to an emergency halt.

"Right, you get off now, please — quickly, quickly," said Subramaniam as Geoff dropped down onto the track to receive the hand luggage and assist Sarah with what was a five-foot drop.

The indignant conductor waved his flag, a green one this time, blew his whistle and the train moved off. Sarah looked about her. She guessed that they were about a quarter of a mile out of Kajang Station and all she could see were trees and the train disappearing to the North. She turned to Geoff who was gathering together the hand luggage and looking furious.

"Wouldn't it have been better to have continued the journey to KL and get a taxi back?" she asked.

He appeared to be choosing his words carefully.

"That man at the station is our estate manager, he is one of the most senior managers in the company — indeed in the country. He has been meeting the train over the past three days expecting us to be on it. To say that he is displeased would be putting it mildly — he's *bloody livid.*

"So how do you imagine it would be if we disappeared for a fourth day?"

"You mean we shouldn't have had those three days in Singapore?"

"Exactly, but on the other hand we received no instructions to proceed directly from the ship to the train and to Kajang. Tickets have to be booked."

Sarah looked around her. On either side of the track there was scorched scrub and *lallang* (grass) beyond which there were rows and rows of trees and looking back she realised that they were quite some way from the town. The shoes she was wearing were quite unsuitable and the cream sharkskin dress recently bought in Singapore had not been designed for jumping out of trains. The straight skirt which buttoned down one side now had a revealing slit exposing more leg and thigh than was considered correct. The buttons had shot off when she descended from the train and there was just nothing that she could do about it — perhaps if she carried some hand luggage on that side it wouldn't be noticed. Not that there was anyone to notice anything at the moment.

"Well, we can't just stand here: we'd better set off up the track towards town," said Geoff as he grabbed the heavier items of hand baggage. "You go ahead and as soon as you see somebody — ask for a taxi."

"But I don't speak the language, how can I make them understand?" argued Sarah.

"For God's sake, they all understand the word 'taxi,'" he snapped.

Sarah picked up her case in her left hand to hide the exposed thigh and her umbrella was in her right as she set off carefully picking her way along the line of sleepers rather than the coarse chippings on either side of the track. She thought that she must have looked ridiculous: she certainly felt so. Whatever had possessed her to travel with the umbrella? It could have so easily gone with the baggage. Its elegant long line and gold and black handle had looked good at home in

England but here it was totally out of place.

She was approaching a level crossing and there was a timbered building set back from the road. Its paintwork was cream and black and a flag pole stood before it. The words *"Pejabat Pos"* led her to believe it was a post office, which it was. Suddenly Sarah was aware of children appearing as if from nowhere gathering round her, their cheerful smiling faces and bright white teeth she would long remember.

"Tabek Mem, Tabek!"

She looked at them and mustered a smile in response. She didn't feel like smiling — her feet were killing her, her clothes were sticking to her and the sun was beating down.

"Taxi?" she ventured.

"Ada," came the reply followed by *"Nanti Sini."*

One boy stepped forward, gestured towards the side of the road where there was some shade and then ran off behind the Post Office. Within seconds he was back followed by what looked like an ancient black Morris car at the wheel of which sat an Indian with a big generous smile and bloodshot eyes. He got out and bowed.

"Good afternoon *Mem*, where are you going?"

"To Ulu Tiram Estate," she replied.

The driver positively beamed.

"But I am the taxi driver from Ulu Tiram, I will take you there at once," and he proceeded to start up the engine.

"Wait, my husband!" she interrupted and pointed down the railway line to where Geoff could be seen weighed down with luggage slowly making his way towards them.

"This is terrible, terrible!" said the driver, who, calling some of the young boys to accompany him, ran down the line and in no time at all came back with Geoff, the luggage and a look of triumph.

Luggage finally installed in the boot, they set off for Ulu Tiram. Seated in the back seat Sarah looked at the passing scenery. As they left the edge of the town she was surprised to be stopped at a police checkpoint. The policeman spoke to the driver and then they all looked at its passengers, grinned and waved the car through. This brought home to Sarah that she would be living in a curfew area from now on. Geoff had previously told her about the food denial measures aimed at cutting off supplies to the terrorists and explained that for the local people all tinned food was punctured on purchase and rice rationed. Although this caused some hardship, the population accepted it as a fair means of helping to eradicate terrorism.

In no time at all they turned right off the main road where a large sign indicated the entrance to "ULU TIRAM ESTATE - MANAGER H KING." Sarah noticed what appeared to be a small Hindu shrine with garlands of flowers in an area that was unplanted with trees. She was to learn later that this was where cremations were carried out whenever a member of the Tamil community died.

The entrance road was of red laterite and dusty. They crossed a steel framed bridge where another turning to the right was sign posted "FACTORY and OFFICE." Almost immediately after this and on the left was a garish building, its arched entrance and walls decorated with bright paintings and carvings of animals and human figures. This was the Hindu temple. They were now passing a playing field or *padang* on the other side of which was the estate school. Across the other side of the road were the coolie lines, large dark single-storey buildings surrounded by concrete drains and enveloped in smoke as the evening meals were being prepared. Then, on the same side as the playing fields came the Asian staff bungalows and the dispensary where the estate dresser was at work with evening surgery. People were everywhere, men, women and children. A game of football was taking place on the *padang*, women were cooking food, and children were riding bicycles which were far too big for them. Others were obviously returning from a shop carrying vegetables.

They drove out through a gate in the perimeter fence passing through row after row of rubber trees stretching endlessly into the distance. The estate road was now deserted and Sarah noticed that the cups on the trees to collect latex were all upturned. They were now climbing — they had turned onto a side road and were going round and up a hill. As they neared the top they drove through an open gateway up towards a grand-looking colonial-style house with an *atap* roof, soaring high above which was the reddish orange blossom of a giant Flame of the Forest tree. The house was set in a well laid-out garden with lawns and ablaze with colourful flowering shrubs and trees. Bougainvillaeas grew in profusion contrasting sharply with the yellow Cannas and the frangipanis, gardenias and *bunga rayas* were planted in positions which gave maximum effect.

Sarah commented on the gardens and house and the driver, whose name she had learnt was Sammy Nathan, smiled widely, well-satisfied that this young *mem* was appreciative of her surroundings. Geoff was quiet still, he was not looking forward to renewing his brief acquaintance with his general manager. He had certainly got off on the wrong foot and he had the gut feeling that things would be difficult for a while.

Drawing up under the entrance port, they were greeted by two dogs who rushed out barking furiously. One was a small dachshund which made most of the noise, the other of indeterminate breed had black and white patches, Sarah decided that she preferred the latter. Behind the dogs came Henry King. Geoff introduced Sarah.

Henry King had just downed a stiff Scotch when he heard the taxi arrive. His patience was exhausted. He had objected to an ex-army officer being posted as assistant manager to one of his estate divisions by Head Office. He had voiced his opinion to fellow planters at the Club, and as if to prove him right, this ex-Captain Geoffrey Farrer had stood him up three times in the last three days as he waited like a batman to the confounded fellow at Kajang Station. He didn't like army officers and didn't intend keeping this one on his estate.

Henry had been a lance corporal in The Volunteers when the Japanese invaded Malaya in 1941 and he had ended up a prisoner-of-war or "in the bag" as they called it. He resented the fact that he had not been commissioned but like so many planters and ex-pats he had elected to serve in an all-European unit of The Volunteers rather than as an officer with locally enlisted personnel. He now had an unhealthy chip on his shoulder. *C'est la guerre!* It was a great pity, for fellow ex-POWs had a terrific respect for Henry's spirit as a prisoner; he had endured numerous beatings and other punishment for his stubborn refusal to conform to his captors' demands.

He looked at Sarah in front of him: another problem. Normally assistant managers were unmarried with no permanent distractions from the job.

"Well, come in. I expect you'd like some tea."

He bellowed at the dogs to lie down and then called out for Gopal. Seconds later a grey-haired middle-aged Indian dressed immaculately in white cotton drill shirt and slacks appeared, his manner pleasant if somewhat obsequious. His eyes quickly scrutinised the newcomers before he darted off to get the tea.

In an attempt to make conversation Sarah commented on

the garden.

"Oh yes, the *kebun* is pretty good but my wife has always taken a great interest. She is now in England getting our home up to standard for our retirement next year."

He looked round the large comfortably-furnished lounge.

"Most of our stuff has gone home - Persian rugs and things like that."

They talked for about an hour when it was explained to Geoff that muster was at 5.30am tomorrow, brunch would be at 10.30am and lunch at 1.30pm.

"Staff are expected in the office from 3pm until dismissed," as the manager put it.

"I expect you'd like to go to your room upstairs and freshen up before dinner. Your luggage is already up there."

"Oh, I was going to ask about that. I thought perhaps it was still at the station," Geoff blurted out, anxious not to revive memories of their arrival.

"My driver collected your luggage."

No more was said and they retreated gratefully to their room.

The room was enormous, it overlooked the garden and had windows with shutters opening on to two sides. In the centre of the room hanging from the ceiling was a large electric fan and a big square mosquito net enclosed the twin beds. Between the top of the interior walls and ceiling was open trellis-like woodwork to permit free air passage which was good but consequently the rooms were not soundproof. Geoff suspected that conversation might therefore not be private so they spoke in whispers.

"Let's hope that we get into our own bungalow tomorrow. I find him odd to say the least," said Geoff, who was obviously ill at ease.

Prior to dinner Henry King sank a few generous-sized White Label whiskies and became noticeably more amenable. He explained to Sarah and Geoff that their bungalow was on the Western Division of the Estate. It was new, as was its furniture, but that they would have to wait a few days before they could move in while servants were engaged and special constables posted in to protect them.

CHAPTER III

The following morning Geoff was up for muster at 5am whilst Sarah was left to her own devices at the manager's bungalow. She spent the time admiring the gardens and house and chatting to Gopal, who was a mine of information. By the end of the morning she felt that she knew a great deal about Ulu Tiram Estate and the people associated with it. When Geoff and Henry King returned for breakfast, or "brunch" as he referred to it, plans were made for Sarah and Geoff's move to their bungalow.

Sarah was excited at the prospect of moving into their first home and Geoff keen to put some distance between himself and Mr King. The atmosphere during the morning had not been easy.

"He's an arrogant blighter and has an unhealthy grudge against ex-army officers. I'm finding him bloody difficult to relate to," said Geoff. "I guess I'll just have to keep working at it."

The bungalow turned out to be new, large and airy. It was right on the roadside with a drive in. Geoff was a little concerned at its siting but kept that to himself. The rooms were large and furnished with teak and bamboo furniture and Sarah was delighted. A Malay couple had been engaged to work as *amah* and gardener and lived in a block behind the bungalow together with four special constables (SCs) and their wives. These SCs were to be their "bodyguards", one of whom was to accompany Geoff at all times when working about the estate — three thousand acres of which were now to be directly under his care. The place became a hive of activity as the unpacking of their belongings took place.

Word soon got around that they had moved in and in no time at all the "neighbours" started to call. The first were two other assistant managers on the estate, a Dutchman by the name of Hank van de Gaast and a Frenchman, Mark Lebrun. Hank had an attractive wife, Julie, about the same age as Sarah and also new to Malaya. Sarah hoped that they would become friends. Both their bungalows were on other divisions of the estate and some miles away.

The next to call were Rob and Catrina Ferguson from the neighbouring Puchong Estate who were to become very good friends. Slightly older than Geoff and Sarah they had three little girls. Sarah and Catrina took to each other immediately, each sensing that the other was someone in whom they could confide. The Fergusons had recently moved from an estate in Pahang where they had been ambushed twice and were lucky to be alive, although they both made light of it.

Another caller was a bizarre character called Ray Robinson. He was an Australian and drove up to the bungalow one morning as Sarah and Geoff were breakfasting. It was of course late morning but nevertheless a quiet time to browse through The Straits Times and catch up on what was happening elsewhere. The peace was rudely shattered as a Landrover carrying six SCs, all armed to the teeth, screeched into the drive. At the wheel sat a large burly fellow crowned with a big bush hat. Geoff could not believe what he was seeing: the guy had grenades clipped to his belt and two hanging from a sort of harness, one at each breast. He had a revolver suspended to his right thigh and across the dash board lay a pump action shot gun. He bounded from the vehicle and ran up to the front porch.

"Hi folks, just called to say 'welcome.' Can't stay long, there's a bit of activity in the area, must get back to my place.

My name's Ray. We've a roast suckling pig party on Sunday at noon. Serdau Estate. Must be off — see you there."

Sarah and Geoff just looked at each other. Was that real? They shook their heads not believing what they had just witnessed. Discreet enquiries revealed that Ray and his long-suffering wife Jane were not generally accepted in the community but nevertheless they went along on the Sunday and had a few beers and suckling pig. All was a bit primitive and a very mixed group of people were there. What put Geoff off were the flies — they were everywhere, on everything and in everything. It was a pity really, as Jane was quite nice.

They settled into a daily routine on the estate, Geoff attending muster at 5.30am every day other than Sunday. But down in the labour lines at 4am old Muniandy, once a tapper himself, would ring the temple bell setting in motion Ulu Tiram's working day. This took place in pitch blackness rain or shine, the shrill clanging being impossible to ignore. The sound could even be heard in the Farrers' bungalow if the wind was right, which thank God was not often.

The Tamil labour force in the lines would wake up, clear their throats and set about preparing their breakfast and also a meal of rice to carry out to work to be eaten either when they had finished tapping or at the 11 o'clock statutory break for field workers. If it was raining the temple bell would not be rung again which meant an enforced vacation for the labour force — with no pay. Otherwise the bell was rung, muster took place and people were despatched off into various work tasks for the day. Down in Kajang a similar programme of events took place as the Chinese contract labour would sally forth on their bicycles or on the open contractors' trucks to the estate. The Chinese contractor for Geoff's division was Loh Sek a Hokien. All people leaving Kajang, as with every other community in Malaya, were searched for foodstuffs that could be of use to the CTs. Bicycle frames and wheels were checked to see that no uncooked rice was being smuggled out and of course tinned food had to be punctured.

Each morning Geoff made his way down to the lines for 5.30am. Already the workforce would have assembled to await roll call which was carried out by Indian conductors called *kanganis* (overseers) as well as *mandors* (foremen). Geoff felt somewhat superfluous on these occasions but nevertheless he was expected to be there.

The actual rubber tappers all had fixed allocations of some 350-500 trees for tapping so that without further instruction they returned to the coolie lines to collect their latex buckets and tapping knives which came in two styles: a narrow gouge for "push" tapping or a *jebong*, a type of farrier's knife for "pull" tapping. They also took a bottle of water and a meal with them in a three-tier decorated tin called a tiffin carrier, which held cooked rice, vegetable curry and *sambal* (pickle), as they made their way either independently or by estate transport to their tasks. The tapping was confined to half the circumference of each tree and by a single cut at about 20 degrees slope. The latex was found between the outer corky bark and the living cambium layer. The skilled tapper removed a thin shaving of bark about one millimetre in thickness, taking care not to wound the living cambium layer. Latex flowed down the 20 degree sloped cut and into a vertical channel across which a thin metal spout was fixed to lead the flowing latex into a collecting cup.

The field workers were assigned to the various tasks listed for that day: be it straightforward weeding, road work, draining or whatever. They then had to draw the appropriate stores and be ready to leave on the estate transport at 6am taking them to the place at which they were to work. Geoff would visit all the work going on in his division of the estate, taking the opportunity to use some of the Tamil phrases he had learnt from studying his Wells' Coolie Tamil the previous night. He was expected to pass The Incorporate Society of Planters Tamil Examination in his first year which would earn him an extra ten dollars each month.

Thanks to being able to get personal copies of The Rubber Research Institute Bulletin each month, Geoff soon acquired a deeper interest in the production of rubber than was perhaps the case with some previous assistant managers in their first year. He soon learned to identify the principal root diseases caused by three fungi - *Fomes lignosus, Ganoderma pseudoferreum* and *Fomes noxious*. When he reported to Mr King an outbreak of Pink Disease in the branches and stems of one section of rubber trees on the estate he was told that he hadn't enough years' experience to recognise the condition, but when the estate manager made his own inspection he found there were thirty infected trees.

Within days of Geoff reporting the Pink Disease, Henry King decided that he wanted him to look after the factory. On Ulu Tiram the raw rubber was prepared both as smoked sheet and as pale crêpe (and PNS-Pebbly non skid) for export. The latex collected at the various weighing stations on the estate was brought to the factory by tanker where it was transferred into a bulk container for dilution with water to give a solution of about 15per cent rubber content. It was then transferred into large aluminium lined wooden tanks where, having added the coagulant, normally formic acid, aluminium spacers were slotted in about 1.5 inches apart. The coagulated rubber formed into soft slabs which were then rolled out into thin sheets by passing them successively through a battery of five or six pairs of even-speeded rollers to give progressively increasing "nips." The sheets were then dried and smoked in a smokehouse for about four days. The smokehouse was a single-storey building divided into compartments so that each day's crop of wet rubber was kept separate. The sheets were hung on trolleys in the factory and having drained for some time were pushed into the compartments for drying and smoking. The smokehouse was operated by burning old rubber trees in a wood-burning furnace from which flues carried hot air and smoke into the drying-house chambers. The smoking or "kippering" served as an antiseptic against mould during transit. Crêpe rubber went through a somewhat different process.

At about 11 o'clock Geoff returned to his bungalow each morning for breakfast. Officially he was allowed 30 minutes, just enough time for a quick cuddle and a hasty bacon and eggs. Sarah never ceased to marvel at his appetite. Geoff very rarely had time to glance at more than the headlines of his daily paper, The Malay Mail. Then it was out to the field again to supervise the tappers and the weeders until about 1.30pm or to the factory to prepare to receive the day's latex.

One morning he opened the paper to see the headline:

'TERROR OF LIPIS' IS DEAD: ONE OF FIVE LEADERS KILLED IN PAHANG

Blackmail papers found on his body

Kuala Lumpur, Wed. – Wuh Pun, the English-educated "Terror of Lipis" is dead – and according to an official spokesman there are many people in the districts of Kuala Lipis, Raub and Bentong who can

> now sleep more easily. Full details of how he met his death are being withheld in the interest of security but documents concerning his blackmail transactions were found on his body.

The report went on to list four other Leaders killed the previous weekend, one of whom was with Wuh Pun when he was killed.

Geoff let out a yell of triumph as Sarah rushed in from the bedroom to see what had happened.

"Got the bastard at last!" he shouted. "We tracked him for over a year until I returned to England. He seemed to have a charmed life. The locals were led to believe that he could only be killed by a silver bullet."

"Who was he? Why is he so important to you?'" asked Sarah.

Geoff hesitated — he had previously told Sarah only a little of the shooting which involved a female terrorist. He now told her in detail, and how he had been ill at ease since the happening. Now at last, he felt that chapter in his life was all over.

That afternoon he was on a "high" and was delighted when Rob Ferguson telephoned and asked them both to pop over to their estate that evening for what was referred to as a "Pre-Curfew *Stengah.*" The curfew was from 7pm to 5.30am and no movement was supposed to take place except in areas designated as being "white" i.e. cleared of terrorism. An area bordered by the back road to Kuala Lumpur through Serdang was about to be declared "grey" but Ulu Tiram Estate was still a "black" area where full restrictions were in force.

As stated, no movement after 7pm was the rule. Rules of course are often broken and that night was no exception. Rob and Geoff polished off a bottle of scotch and a few Anchor Beers as they laughed and chatted away. Sarah and Catrina had a couple of G&Ts as they too engaged in conversations about this one and that one and then went upstairs to see Catrina's latest purchases of dresses which had come through Polly Peck's mail order that morning. In no time at all it was 11.20pm and they rose to say goodnight.

Returning to Ulu Tiram along the estate roads in the armour plated khaki-coloured short wheelbase Landrover was an eerie experience. One could so easily imagine all manner of things: the rubber trees were ghostly and white in the headlights as Geoff drove peering through the visor cut out in the armour-plated windscreen. Sarah's imagination led her to thoughts of tigers and she often claimed to have seen eyes lit up in the dark. Geoff knew that almost anyone or anything would be more than likely blinded by their powerful spotlight. Anyway CTs rarely moved at night, in his experience.

When they had settled in on the estate Geoff joined The Volunteers, or more correctly The Federation of Malaya Volunteer Force (Recce Corps), and was given command of 'A' Company with platoons at both Seremban and Malacca where each Sunday he attended parades. He had no sooner taken command of the Company when a new Permanent Staff Instructor was posted to them. Geoff was absolutely delighted when it turned out to be none other than ex-Corporal Hamid, now a Company Sergeant Major. Hamid too was delighted: they had spent so much time together on very active service. They had a bond which could never be broken.

Henry King was inwardly furious, but Head Office in Kuala Lumpur gave their full support, one of its directors being a former Commanding Officer of the Battalion. What really got under Henry King's skin was the frequent arrival of Hamid on his motorcycle at the estate office during afternoon administration. He would step into the outer office, salute Geoff and hand over despatches, orders for signature and other Volunteer matters. To CSM Hamid MM the other people in the office appeared to be of no consequence. Major Farrer was his commander and he alone.

Hamid bin Haji Ali was born in Kampong Ulu Dong, Raub in 1920. He had joined the Malay Regiment in 1940 and had been stationed at Dungun in Trengganu where there had been some friction with Japanese employed at the Iron mine at Bukit Besi. Before the Japanese invasion of Malaya he had been transferred to the newly-formed 2nd Battalion in 1941. When the Japanese invaded he was at Kuala Krai in Kelantan and his unit fought a rearguard action down the railway line through Gua Musang and to Lipis. Eventually his Battalion reached Singapore and he was still fighting the Japanese at Jurong when the surrender took place.

The Commanding Officer at a final parade told the troops that they had fought hard and well, that the British would return and when that happened they should report for duty.

Hamid eventually reached Benta in Pahang where he was conscripted into the Japanese Kempetai (police) probably because being aware of his military service they wanted to keep an eye on him. One day in 1945 he overheard that a British officer had landed by parachute and was leading local forces against the Japanese near Padang Tunku. Without any hesitation Hamid gathered three rifles and absconded, and eventually to the surprise of that British officer reported for duty as he had been ordered in 1942.

He rejoined the Malay Regiment when it reformed in 1946 at Port Dickson and was awarded the Military Medal in 1953.

Sarah at this time had managed to get a post with the

Rubber Research Institute and was adjusting well to her new lifestyle. Social life was improving as they made new friends and they had joined the Selangor Club or "The Dog" as it was known. Things were going really well — Geoff had made contact with his old Battalion and invitations were being received weekly to various parties and functions. They had bought a second-hand A70 car and he had quite taken to the work of a planter.

It was a Friday night and Geoff was seated at his desk in the lounge doing his weekly report while Sarah was devoting some time to herself. She had just finished washing her hair when there was a sudden unmistakable burst of gunfire. Startled, she wrapped a towel around her wet head and made for the lounge, expecting to see Geoff, just as the lights went out. He was at the back of the house directing the Special Constables to positions of defence. He saw Sarah appear on the steps.

"Get back into the bathroom, lie flat in the bath and stay there! It's the safest place. I think we are under attack," he shouted.

She did as she was told, while Geoff lifted the phone and called Kajang Police. All was then quiet, even the crickets, frogs and mosquitoes became silent.

She heard Geoff's voice: "Do not fire unless you see a target." He was speaking to the SCs. She felt happier now Geoff was obviously in control.

There was another burst of fire and the bedroom balcony was peppered with bullets. Sarah suddenly remembered that Rob and Catrina had gone that evening to the cinema in KL and had left their children with the *amah* and police at their bungalow. It was the first time that they had ever done so. They had a special permit.

"My God!" thought Sarah, "They may have been ambushed at the junction."

She eased herself gingerly out of the bath and crawled to the front of the bungalow. Geoff was there.

"Get back in the bath, Sarah!" he snapped.

"Geoff — Catrina and Rob are at the cinema tonight, do you think they might have been ambushed? What about the kids?"

"The police know. Now get back!"

There was another burst of fire as Geoff threw himself on top of Sarah, his gun at the ready as two SCs announced themselves at the back entrance.

"*Tuan*, listen — vehicles are coming."

Geoff listened.

Within seconds an armoured truck drove up to the bungalow and a Police Lieutenant sprang out.

"Nothing to worry about!" he announced. "There's a flying fox shoot on the Serdang Road — it came a bit close, that's all. They were celebrating the area becoming classified as 'grey.'"

Geoff could not believe his ears.

"Bollocks!" he stormed and shone his torch on the bungalow. "How the hell do you account for this, then?"

The veranda was riddled with bullets. Without any order the police who had all dismounted from the vehicle darted for cover.

"Get up, you fools!" shouted Geoff. "Whoever did this will be well away by now."

Next morning at first light a police jungle squad arrived with tracker dog and having seen the damage in daylight scoured the estate for signs of the enemy. They discovered that only one weapon appeared to have been used and the tracker dog, having picked up the scent, led them through the estate to a place about two miles up the Serdang Road where it appeared the attacker had mounted a motorcycle and driven off.

A Special Branch Officer came to see Geoff and announced: "It would seem that someone has it in for you."

This information was passed on to Henry King and the fact that it was virtually impossible to defend the bungalow, leaving Mr and Mrs Farrer as sitting ducks for any would-be assassin, left him no option but to move them to another old bungalow on the Eastern Division which was more secure, being on the hilltop and well protected by a security fence and perimeter lighting. For the next few days the district buzzed with speculation about the attack and people became more security-conscious.

CHAPTER IV

The bungalow was situated on a hilltop above that of the manager's, at the end of the road which passed by his entrance. It had its disadvantages, because Henry King had at some time built a type of cattle grid over the small culvert which went under and across the road at that point. It rattled loudly whenever a vehicle went over it — consequently he knew whenever his assistant manager came in or out. In other respects the bungalow was ideal, perched on the hilltop, with panoramic views over much of the estate save where a jungle covered re-entrant ran up to the north side and through which ran the water pipe bringing their water. It was forced up by an hydraulic ram pumping water from a small pond of beautifully clear and cold water not far away from the weighing shed to where tappers brought their latex each day to be weighed and tested for dry rubber content. The bungalow was considerably older than their previous one but it had a certain charm. It was furnished with good quality teak furniture and one could get a breeze through its doors and windows at almost any time, although it was a bit 'dicey' when the occasional tropical thunderstorm took place. Then all doors and *tingkaps* (shutters) had to be bolted. Glass windows were not in use.

No sooner had they moved in than Taleb and Zainon the cook and gardener gave their notice. They were very apologetic about it, but the curfew and the restrictions on foodstuffs and movement were too much and they moved back to Kampong Bahru in Kuala Lumpur.

Sarah was grateful that a new electric cooker had been installed for her. In the bungalow that they had just left she had had to manage with a wood burning Dover Stove which although it no doubt had many virtues was not ideal for her in that hot climate. It also gave off a great deal of smoke. Her refrigerator was kerosene-burning because electricity from their generator was not available for twenty-four hours each day. Ants and mosquitoes were a problem but, strangely enough, not flies. There was a permanent battle with ants which arrived in columns whenever sugar or anything sweet was dropped on the floor. The food safe which was also fly-proof had to stand in bowls (or cigarette tins) containing kerosene. The kitchen was not the place for a planter's wife and so Sarah resolved to visit the Domestic Agency in KL at the earliest opportunity, where she would get an English speaking *amah*.

She had been learning to speak Bahasa Melayu for some time but she found it a slow process and her lack of fluency had led to frustration and mistakes in the house. She would never forget the look on Taleb's face when she was telling him to lock the front and rear doors each night, she told him:

"Malam malam kenching sini kenching sana."

Unfortunately she had muddled *kenching* (pee) for *kunchi* (lock) and in effect was ordering him each night to pee here and pee there.

The week following their move she called in at the agency.

The likely candidates were seated on a bench under a slowly rotating overhead fan. They were not an impressive group but one did stand out among the others. She was clean, tidy and spoke quite good English. She claimed that she had worked for a tin miner for a number of years until he retired to UK. She was not at all shy and seemed at ease and eager to please.

"Will you mind the loneliness of the rubber estate?" asked Sarah.

"No, no, *Mem*. I am used to a tin mine and living away from the town. All I want is one day and night off each week to visit my mother. I shall be quite happy."

They agreed on the matter of rate of pay and Sarah set off in the car, her new *amah* seated beside her. They called at a Chinese house where the *amah* picked up a case of belongings. They then drove back to the estate, Sarah feeling well satisfied with her acquisition, and already planning how to restore the bungalow to an orderly state.

When she drove up to the bungalow Geoff was there waiting.

"What kept you?" He was abrupt and cast a look of almost displeasure in the direction of the Chinese *amah*.

"You like to see my references, Sir?" she asked.

He nodded, accepting the outstretched bundle of paper.

"What is your name?"

"Loh Mai," she replied, flashing a brilliant smile in his direction.

Sarah wondered how much her front gold teeth had cost her.

Geoff sat down to study the references while Sarah showed Loh Mai to her quarters at the back of the bungalow. When she returned Geoff looked none too pleased.

"I don't like her. Why didn't you get a Malay?" he asked.

"There weren't any there: it's not easy to find an English speaking servant."

"To hell with speaking English, you are learning Malay!"

With that he stormed out of the bungalow went down the steps to the parked Landrover. She heard him rattle over the cattle grid as he drove off to the office.

An uneasy truce existed in the bungalow: Loh Mai was on trial. Geoff felt sure that she had been the mistress of this tin miner who had provided the reference. Her familiarity shown in front of male visitors made him even more certain of it. In addition he suspected that something was going on at the back with Ah Choy, his one and only Chinese special constable, the other five being Malay.

"It's bad for discipline and control and the Malays won't like it," he told Sarah.

Loh Mai's cooking turned out to be quite good and because they both suspected that Sarah was pregnant they kept the *amah* on, at least until they could find someone more suitable.

Christmas was approaching and returning from her work at the RRI one day Sarah was met by Loh Mai obviously in some excitement.

"Come see *Mem*, come, come."

Sarah followed her to the back of the bungalow.

"Contractor, he come, bring many gifts."

She pointed to her shower door which Sarah cautiously opened to be greeted by a chorus of sounds. There were hens, cockerels, ducks and guinea fowl, all shrieking and flapping in panic. She slammed the door tight.

"My goodness, what are we to do with them?"

"Klismas *Mem*, big party."

She took Sarah's arm and said: "*Mem* come see — more, more," and in the room off the kitchen there were three cases of whisky, cigarettes, brandy, chocolates and a solitary Christmas pudding tinned and manufactured in Liverpool!

When Geoff came home later Sarah greeted him with the news.

"Are we allowed to accept gifts from the contractor?" she asked.

"Yes, sure, but only at Christmas, not at any other time."

Having taken stock of everything they decided that the

guinea fowls and ducks were in excess of their needs. Sarah wondered if they could sell them without causing offence. They were not rolling in money and could do with a little extra cash at this time. Ah Choy the SC was consulted and after a great deal of thought they decided to take the ducks and guinea fowls out of the shower, get them into the Landrover to be sold at the local market.

Ah Choy opened the shower door to grab the birds for sale but as he did so the whole captive flock burst out of the shower, fled into the garden eventually settling in the branches of a large tree where they stayed. The ducks and the guinea fowl were speedily rounded up and were duly sold. Getting the others down as and when they were required for the pot proved to be quite a pantomime.

Christmas came and went. It had been a quiet one for them as Sarah had been unwell in the early stages of pregnancy and had enforced bed rest for a week. On Christmas Day however she had been up and about looking forward to a traditional dinner. Although it was a quiet time for them they were in good spirits — there was the baby to look forward to in the early summer and in the meantime there was young Gerry to keep them busy.

Gerry was a delightful golden labrador pup that Geoff had given Sarah before Christmas and was a source of great happiness. He would accompany Geoff in the Landrover when he went on his rounds and the rest of the time he was in the bungalow tearing apart whatever took his fancy. By Christmas he was reasonably house-trained and was content to chew an old slipper of Geoff's, contentedly lying at his feet as they sipped their pre-dinner drinks.

Suddenly there was an appalling commotion from the direction of the kitchen. Both Loh Mai and Ah Choy were shouting and screaming and the door burst open as they crashed into the lounge.

"What the hell's going on?" bellowed Geoff.

Both of them were a sight to behold, splattered in Christmas pudding. Loh Mai was hysterical as she proceeded to give Ah Choy the benefit of her wrath.

"Your fault, not mine. You spoil *Mem*'s Klismas Dinner, you stupid, *lopong*. I stupid let you help me."

The tirade then switched into Chinese while poor Ah Choy stood there covered in pudding and obviously in some pain.

Geoff took him back into the kitchen and tried to clean him up with cold water. The stuff was everywhere, in his hair, eyes, ears and face. His clothing did not matter.

"Sorry, *Tuan*. I opened the tin too soon and it exploded."

Geoff was not happy about the SC's eyes and bundled Ah Choy into the Landrover, telling Sarah: "Hope I shan't be long, I'm taking him to the hospital."

"Well, that will give Henry King something to think about!" thought Sarah, as they drove down the hill, rattling the cattle grid as they went by.

Sarah settled down in an armchair with a fresh drink to await Geoff's return while Loh Mai set about clearing up the mess. Nothing could be salvaged of the pudding but Gerry found it to his liking and it was soon cleared up.

Loh Mai was still furious with Ah Choy and equally so with some of the other SCs who had emerged from their quarters to see what all the fuss was about. They did not care for her very much and she slammed the doors and shutters without more ado.

Geoff and Ah Choy were away for about an hour. Kajang Hospital had been quiet as one would have expected on Christmas night and he had been seen to straight away. There were no problems with his eyes and when they returned to the bungalow Ah Choy went directly to his SC quarters without speaking to Loh Mai. Dinner was eventually served and despite the upheaval was surprisingly good, although Sarah did miss the pudding.

From then on Ah Choy and Loh Mai were no longer the best of friends and this gave Geoff the opportunity to get rid of her. She developed a new friendship with one of the Chinese sub-contractors and when Geoff discovered her "entertaining" him in her quarters during the day when Sarah was out and he returned on foot she was instantly dismissed. He paid her up to date, gave two weeks extra and drove her back to KL. When Sarah came home she found Geoff looking very pleased with himself and no sign of Loh Mai.

"It's all right, Sarah, we have a new *amah* coming tomorrow; tonight we are going to The Dog."

Sarah loved going to The Dog. It was essentially a meeting place as well as having the facilities — that always made it a pleasure to visit. It was a second home to members coming in from outstation, somewhere to freshen up, have lunch or dinner and then settle back into its relaxing cane furniture. *Stengahs* — whisky sodas — or ice-cold Anchor or Tiger Beer were served by the "boys" as the waiters were called and chits signed for entry into the members' accounts which were paid monthly. The dining room and the standard of food served were first class and the general atmosphere relaxing. A unique large mural the length of the dining room wall depicted the Battle of Britain which most found rather strange but interesting.

There were of course the more hectic and social occasions such as St Andrew's Night, Burns' Night and St George's Night and more recently they had danced the night away after enjoying a most entertaining floor show of Hindu Ballet. It had been a remarkable demonstration of agility with its strange (to Western eyes) exact but often quite incomprehensible signs and conventions, with every movement of wrists and fingers, every bodily attitude having a definite significance. The manager of the club, a Pole, unbeknown to the attentive audience had donned the rich and colourful attire of the dancers and somehow mastered the ardent looks and gestures of the professionals. He joined with them in part of the show, finishing with a solo performance before revealing his true identity to the spell bound club members. The applause was unbelievable.

On this occasion they made their way to the small bar beyond the dining room where they intended to have a quiet drink and order their meal. To their surprise who should be perched on a stool at the bar but Terry Harris one of their fellow passengers on *The Oranje*, who had previously been to Singapore where he had done his National Service as an officer in the RASC. He was now a planter up North and was alone and delighted to see Sarah and Geoff. Several drinks later they moved into the dining room to continue their exchange of news over dinner.

Terry was very happy on his estate and got on extremely well with his manager, a fellow Scot. Geoff told him of his less fortunate position but said that things were about to change because Henry King was due to retire and his replacement was much pleasanter person altogether. Terry's estate was at Tanjong Malim and when they parted company they promised to make the trip North to see him in the not too distant future.

Geoff had always kept himself fit and occasionally he managed to get away from the estate and go cross-country running with the Hash-House Harriers. This name seemed to crop up all over the Colonial world wherever young men joined together to run for fun. In Kuala Lumpur it appeared to be a very loose-knit association where one turned out in one's running kit at the appointed RV and ran over the route mapped out or followed the 'hare' who marked the way with a paper trail. Members took it in turn to provide ice-cold beer served from the boots of their cars at the finish — which of course was the same place as the start.

Nobody was prepared for what happened in March of that year. The runners met near to the Military Cemetery on the outskirts of KL on the road to Cheras. There was a very good turn-out and three "hares" were selected to lay a paper chase over what seemed to be a reasonable route passing through some neglected rubber estate land, some *belukar* (secondary jungle) behind the cemetery and some cultivated land used by vegetable growers. The "hares" set off and the pack waited for about half an hour until they were sure that all the likely runners had arrived. Then they set off in hot pursuit.

The three "hares", running at a leisurely pace, had just entered the *belukar*, which was not too difficult, when they crossed a small stream. Running on the far bank they became aware that the ground beneath their feet was swept clean and then Tom Mallory, one of the "hares", yelled to the others "Run like shit!" which they did — for they had run straight into a Communist Terrorist camp. Luckily for them it was unoccupied except for two females and a male guard who was covering the opposite side from where they had entered. The "hares" ran till they were breathless; they stopped, listened and decided that they were not being followed. The three had no time to discuss what had happened — they would do that later and no doubt for the rest of their lives. The important thing at that moment was to stop the following pack before they ran into the now-alerted terrorists.

They quickly calculated that if they ran due West from their present position for about five minutes and then South South East they could re-cross their route. They were scared stiff as they ran but even more so about the danger to their friends, even now running to their deaths. As they ran, the terrain seemed to be much more difficult and as they stumbled along, their eyes straining, they looked for the paper trail and signs of the Communists ahead. Luck was with them twice that day for they found the trail and had no sooner done so when the first two runners in the pack came running towards them. Quickly they moved back to the start. Tom Mallory got into his car and drove to the nearest telephone to report what had happened. He then returned to the others to find them all laughing and drinking as the other two "hares" related over and over again what had happened, the story gaining extra detail with each telling. Tom joined in the laughter describing how he had seen two female terrorists, looking more startled than himself, cooking at a fire as he burst into their camp. He claimed to have seen one of them go for her rifle but nobody could recall hearing any shots.

A Landrover pulled in beside them and a young Malay officer with seven men got out. He spotted Geoff whom he recognised and went straight to him. Geoff called Tom across and the full story was told before the subaltern and his party moved off to investigate further. It was very unlikely that they would find the CTs still there — probably they would have fled to a previously chosen R.V.

There was always the danger that they might ambush the route in. As expected however the patrol found the camp deserted so they withdrew leaving a three-man ambush behind for the next 24 hours. Early the next morning two unsuspecting CTs unwittingly walked into the ambush party, who shot one and captured the other. That night at The Dog the Harriers had a celebration that left many a sore head the next morning.

The Scots, the Irish and the Welsh are well known to celebrate their patron saints' feast days but the English are as a rule far less nationalistic in these matters. Maybe because they too were a minority race in Malaya they had a thriving branch of the Royal Society of St George who met at the Lake Club. Each year on or about St.George's Night on April 23rd a Ball was held to which the leaders of the other three tribes were invited. Geoff had somehow got himself landed with the organising of the "ceremonial", presumably on account of his military connections. On this occasion he recruited two army chefs in full rig, three trumpeters from the 13th 18th Royal Hussars in No 1 Dress and two Warrant Officers, one a Devon and the other a Seaforth. These two stalwarts were kitted up as Yeomen of the Guard with mock black beaver headgear with red and white cockades around the crown, bright red cloth tunics, breeches and hose, black and yellow braiding, gold emblazonry and pleated white lawn ruffs. They had red garters and black shoes with red and white rosettes and white gloves. Each wore a sword and carried a gold tasselled lance and looked fantastic as they flanked the President of the Royal Society as he welcomed the guests at the entrance.

When everyone had arrived and taken up their seats in the dining-room the first two courses were served. When everyone had finished the three trumpeters entered smartly and sounded a fanfare. Then to the strains of "The Roast Beef of Old England" the Beefeaters (Yeomen of the Guard) escorted the Baron of Beef carried on a stretcher across their shoulders by the two chefs to a side table beside the President who then took wine with them before carving a first ceremonial slice. It was then taken out to the kitchens where presumably there was another which they had prepared earlier for no sooner had the huge joint entered one door than trays of sliced prime English beef came forth out of another.

The meal then continued after which there were the usual speeches welcoming the guests — one of whom replied on behalf of the others — all of which were good-humoured and full of fun setting the scene for the rest of the evening which went on into the early hours. Geoff left Sarah with their guests during the speeches to make sure that the Beefeaters, the trumpeters and the two chefs had been fed and had a few drinks. They had, and they had obviously received plenty of the latter! However, the Beefeaters had disappeared with their outfits which were supposed to have been handed in. Geoff had visions of two drunken Beefeaters armed with sword and lance moving through the city of Kuala Lumpur's streets, being arrested and all appearing in the next day's newspapers. In fact all they did was go back to the Sergeants' Mess in their outfits for a bit of a lark.

When Geoff got back to his wife and guests the dancing was about to start, beginning with the old English "Sir Roger de Coverley" which members of the committee had been taught only the night before. Soon the dancers were into the more usual quicksteps, fox-trots and the like and time just rushed by until Richard, one of the guests, suggested that everyone moved to the swimming club to continue the party through to lunch the next day, which was a Sunday. There were no dissenters — anyway they were already well into Sunday.

Diving into the cool waters of the pool came as quite a shock to the overheated bodies but in no time at all they were all feeling much refreshed. It was the first time that Geoff had seen Richard swim. Despite being disabled in one leg through polio he swam like a fish. His wife and the other two guests all worked at the Rubber Research Institute in Ampang Road together with Sarah and they unlike the Farrers were club members. At about 5am the ground maintenance staff started up their lawn mowers and shortly after that the first waiters appeared and took orders for breakfast which were served at about 7am. As the day moved along the bar opened and they elected to have "a hair of the dog", each of them having a brandy ginger. By midday they were all back to normal preparing for a massive curry lunch before returning to their respective homes.

CHAPTER V

The following Sunday they had accepted an invitation from one of Geoff's old friends, a planter in Pahang, to go over for Curry Tiffin, preceded by a rafting party on the Sungei Bentong. They set out early by car from the estate, driving through KL and on to Bentong via the Genting Pass taking the road from there towards Tras and Tranum. They were early when they reached Shanghai Pahang Estate and were shown in to the manager's bungalow by two Malay boys. Sarah was flabbergasted to see large mousetraps on each of the easy chairs and having a fear of such creatures she sat by the doorway prepared to run should one make an appearance. No sooner had they sat down when a Landrover drew up, out from which jumped a bewhiskered gent who reminded her of one of "the two types" in those wartime cartoons. He wore Chukka boots, fine cotton cord khaki trousers, and a check shirt, and hastened into the room.

"Terribly sorry, been down to the river with some beer, keeps it nice and cold for the finish."

Geoff got up, saying: "Alan, you haven't met Sarah, my wife."

Alan stepped forward taking her hand with a smile.

"Don't know how you came to choose him, a fine-looking girl like you. I wish I were younger." He added wistfully: "I didn't marry, you know."

Sarah smiled and told Alan that she had heard so much about him and of his many lucky escapes from ambushes in the early days when Geoff was stationed in Pahang. She then mentioned rather shyly what had been worrying her from the moment of her arrival.

"Do you have a lot of trouble with mice?"

Alan roared with laughter.

"Good God no, they're to keep the damned dogs off the chairs. They think they own the place! I've put them in the garage today."

Just then an armoured Landrover drew up outside followed by a small convoy of cars. Alan's guests had arrived — they had all met up at the Club and then driven to the estate. The leading vehicle was driven by an Irish planter whom Alan introduced as Haji O'Sullivan. He later told Sarah that Damien, for that was his first name, had become a Muslim (*sudah masok melayu)* and had been on the Haj pilgrimage to Mecca.

"Strange business really. It is strongly rumoured that his older brother is a Jesuit priest. Don't know what they make of it all back in Ireland."

When everyone had been introduced the party moved off in estate vehicles down to the Sungei Bentong where some six or more rafts had been prepared for the race. They were built with bamboo poles lashed together with vines. Geoff paired off with another chap and grinned at Sarah saying: "I'll see you at the finish, dear, if all goes well."

He looked just a little worried, she wondered if he had done this before. The rafts lined up across the river with their crews, and only then did Geoff notice that some had enlisted the help of the Malays to travel with them.

The water was crystal-clear as they started off. The river was wide but gradually narrowed and the current speeded up as they swept along precariously balanced, feet apart and poles at the ready. Shrieks of mock terror came from the leading raft as it disappeared round a bend in the river into a narrow channel of contrasting white water which cascaded over the rocks on either side. The banks were steep and creepers hung down from what was jungle above.

They eventually reached calmer waters and approached a white sandy beach where the estate Landrovers which had made the less hazardous journey were waiting with those guests who did not go rafting. Sarah was watching two *burong rajah udang* (Kingfishers) as they swept by. Their colour fascinated her although she had an inherent dislike of birds close to. The birds had been feasting on grass-hoppers which were in abundance in the long grass above the sandbank and they let out a maniacal cry as they sped off upstream. She was envious of the rafters who looked as though they had enjoyed themselves immensely. She would have loved to have taken part but that would have been most irresponsible as her baby was due in two months' time.

Cold beer from the river was passed around by the men and gin and tonic was offered to the ladies. The rafting had certainly broken the ice considering that very few of the party had met one an other before and they were now chatting away freely.

Among the more interesting of the guests was John Patch, a District Intelligence Officer who had met Geoff previously. He mentioned that he had been present at the interrogation of a surrendered terrorist Liew Kim and in reading up the history of the two men killed by him Geoff's name had come up in connection with one of them, Wuh Pun. This was the first time that Geoff had heard of how he had been killed — by one of his own men. His first reaction was "what a miserable lot, still, I'm glad it's finished."

He said to John: "I suppose you know that I had tracked him for over a year without success?"

John nodded. Geoff momentarily cast his mind back to the killing of Ah Loy. He then heard a voice. It was Alan's.

"You add did well at the rafting, particularly the ladies. Well done. Now if you will get into the transport we will go back to the bungalow and start the second phase."

Everyone moved quickly to the vehicles, especially those who had been rafting who were both wet and anxious for a change of clothing. The ladies looked somewhat the worse for wear and no doubt wanted to repair the damage. Still everyone was in good spirits and looking forward to lunch.

It was one o'clock when they drew up at the bungalow and the tantalising smell of curry wafted in on the breeze. Gradually the circle of chairs (minus the mouse traps) was occupied as people emerged from the bedrooms looking like their former selves. House boys circled with the drinks and prawn crackers and the rafters were soon ringing with laughter. Time just flew by and it was almost four o'clock when they moved into the dining room for lunch.

The spread was fantastic. Laid out in the centre of the table were three large grilled fish (*ikan bawal*) garnished with lettuce leaves and the pink flowers of the Honululu Creeper which grew on the outside of the bungalow. *Sambals* or side dishes were spread about the table in small bowls containing coconut, banana, pineapple, hard-boiled eggs, mango chutney, lime pickle, chillies, sliced cucumber and fried *ikan bilis* (a type of anchovy). These were essentially to cool down curries that were spicy and hot. The house boys came in carrying boiled rice piled high on trays lined with large green banana leaves followed by various curries: Beef *rendang* (a spicy dryish curry), chicken curry (*ayam berempah*), a vegetable curry of Ladies Fingers (*kachang bendi*) and really hot prawn *sambal* (*udang goreng berempah*).

The feast went on as did the cross table conversation until the consumers were defeated. One of the waiters beamed at

Geoff (the buzz having gone around the kitchen that he was ex-Malay Regiment) *"Sudah Kenyang Tuan?"* and he replied *"Sudah, terimah Kaseh."*

The sweet course followed and traditionally it *was Gula Malacca*, a cold sago served with two sauces, coconut cream, and *gula* syrup made from the crystallised sap of coconut palm trees sometimes called Chinese brown sugar. It was both delicious, sweet and soothing. Eventually after coffee for those who wanted it, the party broke up and dispersed, Geoff and Sarah driving back to Kajang after a most enjoyable but exhausting day.

On the way back Geoff told Sarah of his conversation with John Patch and of the bizarre way in which Wuh Pun had met his death. It seemed that a rubber planter from Karak had picked up a Chinese bloke limping along the road who flagged him down. He sized up the situation at once and drove straight to Bentong Police Station where the man, whose name was Liew Kim, told a strange and somewhat blood-curdling story. He wanted to surrender. He had been body-guard to District Committee Member Lim Meng and was moving through the jungle together with Wuh Pun. They had camped overnight on the fringe of the jungle where they could hear traffic on the main road beyond the rubber estate. He told the police interrogator that his weapons and those of his two comrades were hidden in the undergrowth near to where he had hacked them to death with his *parang*.

He was kitted up with jungle green clothing and the next morning in a highly nervous state led a police jungle squad from the place where he had been picked up into the rubber. He eventually found a tree that he had marked with his *parang* from where he soon reached the stream on which he had camped overnight. Liew Kim went straight to where he had hidden the weapons and then upstream to where two bodies lay. The smell was acrid and foul for the bodies were already decomposing. They were lying on the blue plastic sheeting on which they had slept, both bodies badly mutilated and soaked in congealed blood. Flies were everywhere.

The bodies had to be searched and this soon confirmed their identity. Documents included very specific notebooks wrapped in plastic listing people who had been blackmailed and a record of their payments. The officer in charge, being satisfied with the results, ordered the two bodies to be ~~burned~~ buried where they lay and then returned to Bentong with Liew Kim who was rewarded for surrendering, rewarded for the weapons recovered and rewarded for information leading to the death of two terrorists — as they worded it. He was moved to Negri Sembilan, some eight thousand Malayan dollars to the good, to resettle.

CHAPTER VI

The Farrers went to early Mass each Sunday at the local Catholic Church where Fr. LaCroix, a French missionary, was parish priest. He was an amazing man who had spent the war years in China and had some very interesting tales to tell. One late afternoon Geoff had called at his house next door to the church to find him dining with four beggars at his lino-covered table. He heard later that his house was always open to vagrants and beggars to sleep and eat there.

Geoff and Sarah were slightly puzzled when they saw Kupusamy at Mass week after week sitting attentively at the front and staying on for Benediction which sometimes followed. Kupusamy was the young brother of Angeli, a female *kangani* (charge hand) on the estate, a voluptuous Tamil woman who had quite a hold over some of the senior Asian staff. They were all reputed to be deep in her debt for favours bestowed. Also Kupusamy was to be seen regularly round and about the Hindu Temple on the estate.

One day Geoff heard that the Temple Elders had sacked their Brahmin priest because he was too strict and too "high" for them. A new priest was to be installed and all estate staff including the managers and their wives were invited to the official reopening.

On the big day Geoff and Sarah looked in amazement as the new priest resplendent in his robes entered the Temple preceded by a young man swinging a thurible from which the smoke of incense billowed. It was Kupusamy! Behind him came two acolytes ringing handbells, followed by eight people with lit candles on saucers. As Kupusamy passed by he turned and bowed solemnly.

The following morning it was raining heavily and no tapping was being done. The same happened again on the next day and many of the streams were in flood and roads impassable. The rain stopped by mid morning so Geoff and Ah Choy went to KL to collect a new battery. Coming back they were suddenly confronted by the largest turtle that Geoff had ever seen, plumb in the centre of the road. They stopped and approached it. There were Chinese characters painted in red on its shell.

"What does it say?" asked Geoff.

Ah Choy looked very carefully at them and said: "'Longevity to all' — it is a Buddhist saying."

"Where do you think that it belongs, then?" said Geoff.

Ah Choy paused and having thought carefully, replied: "Probably the temple at Sungei Lui. They have turtles there, some are very old and are venerated like gods."

"I think that we should return it to them," said Geoff, "What do you think?"

Ah Choy nodded and so it came to pass that he for the second time that week performed an ecumenical act.

Together they struggled to get the turtle into the back of the Landrover without damaging it or themselves for it was very heavy and only just fitted in. They drove to the temple at Sg Lui where the terraces were laid out at different levels with turtle pools, fish ponds and a formal garden. The recent rains had caused considerable damage and monks — or perhaps they were lay brethren — were engaged in repair work attending to the formal garden and replanting the lily pond.

Geoff and Ah Choy entered into the temple proper where Ah Choy spoke to a saffron-robed monk who was attending to some joss sticks at the feet of a Laughing Buddha, fat and seated on an altar. Geoff could not understand a word of what was going on but he felt intuitively that the monk was not pleased. Ah Choy took the monk out of the temple and Geoff followed. When they got to the Landrover Ah Choy pointed to the turtle and the monk ranted out something and marched back into the temple.

"What did he say?" asked Geoff.

"He is too big, too old and eats too much," replied Ah Choy. "They set him loose on purpose in the flood waters hoping that he would find another place to live."

A Buddhist precept teaches solicitude for all things sentient so it was considered an act of merit to set this creature free. Feeding it is equally meritorious.

When Geoff got back to the bungalow Sarah was out. She had driven over to KL with Julie van de Gaast for her medical check-up and no doubt a visit to the Cold Storage and Robinsons. When she got back late afternoon she parked the car as usual under the carport at the bottom of the steps. Geoff filled her in with an account of his eventful day. Sarah's medical had shown everything to be on course and it had been decided to leave things to carry on for two more weeks and then perhaps consider induction. After dinner they both read for a while and then went to bed.

Sarah woke suddenly, an unfamiliar heavy lurching sound outside the bungalow tensing her every muscle as she grabbed Geoff's arm, saying: "What is it?"

He was listening intently, not to the noise that she had heard but for the sound of human movement. There was none. The lumbering noise continued for a while gradually distancing itself from the bungalow.

By now the SCs could be heard running to their Stand-to Positions and calling out: *"Tuan, tuan, keretah sudah lari!"*

Geoff switched on the powerful perimeter lights, slipped on

his overalls and stepped out of the open window to join his guard. The car had gone, but where to? The gates were still closed. A shout from Kassim who had gone down the garden below the carport, told them that the car had gone that way, crushing through the flower beds and security fence, and disappearing into the darkness of the contoured rows of rubber trees.

Realising that there was nothing sensible that he could do other than inform the police, Geoff turned down the guard leaving two on duty to keep alert and in particular watch the gaping hole in the fence that the car had smashed through. He then telephoned the police, made his report and returned to bed.

They did not sleep further that night but waited till five o'clock when they had some tea and toast.

Geoff went down to the office and made out another report, attended muster then made his way back to the bungalow. Whilst he rounded up two more SCs, two police vehicles arrived and together on foot they traced the route of the car, finding it almost immediately about a hundred yards down from the fence. The bodywork had taken some punishment as it ricocheted between the trees. Having made sure that nothing sinister had been fitted, Geoff got into the driving seat switched on and tried the starter. The engine roared into life as though nothing had happened. He then slowly drove the car through some very difficult terrain onto an estate road.

Here the police had a good look at the car and although it was thought that the incident was accidental and that probably the cold night air had caused contraction of the metal, causing the brakes to release themselves, they took the vehicle away for forensic testing.

The news of the runaway car had obviously spread, resulting in them having an unusual visit in the afternoon. Geoff had just returned from the office and was having a cup of tea with Sarah sitting on the verandah when they became aware that a group of Tamils was coming up the drive chattering excitedly. Their leader stood out as he was dressed somewhat differently from the others who were in their normal attire of *dhoti* and shirt, and there were no women present. The leader, a small man with thick black hair and a greying beard, was wrapped in a long cloak of woven material. The colouring was predominantly purple with grey and red stripes, in his hand he carried a stick resembling a shepherd's crook. Immediately behind him was a young boy of about twelve or thirteen carrying a basket with what looked like three cockerels in it. Their flapping and crowing could be heard above the attendant group who had now started to chant.

Sarah was intrigued

Geoff in the meantime had moved down the steps to the carport to find out what it was all about. The leader moved forward, bowed deeply to Geoff and spoke in a voice that was both obsequious and at the same time warning. His English though hesitant was good.

"Sir, we have come to help you. There is a bad spirit here and because you are a good man and we do not want you to have any more trouble (he cast a knowing eye at the pregnant Sarah) we will sacrifice these three cockerels to appease the spirits. They will cost you only two dollars each."

It took Geoff a moment to stop himself from ordering them off his premises but he gave them the benefit of the doubt and met them half way. Choosing his words carefully he said: "You make your sacrifice if you wish but I have no intention of paying for the cockerels" and with that he turned and took Sarah with him into the bungalow. Once indoors he said to Sarah:

"I'm not paying for their chicken curry tonight." then adding "they are supposed to be vegetarian anyway" as a justification which was not quite true.

"They must think I am bloody stupid."

The dejected members of the little group stood around for a while shaking their heads and muttering in Tamil but finally turned and made their way back in the direction of the coolie lines.

They were not the only visitors that day. Daphne McMillan was next to call. This was quite a surprise as although they knew that she was staying with Rob and Catrina Ferguson she was not officially in the district yet. She was the wife of Tom McMillan who was to be their new manager and was due to take over from Henry King the next week. She had heard about the car and had come to offer Sarah the use of her car and driver should she wish to go to KL for any last-minute shopping for either herself or the baby. This was typical of Daphne as they were to discover.

Geoff went down to Kajang that evening to find out what it was going to cost him to get the car repaired and to call in at the insurance company. The police had not finished with the car — this surprised Geoff somewhat and he wondered what on earth they were expecting to find. As he drove back home he thought how different things would be when the McMillans took over. He was pleased that Sarah seemed to hit it off with Daphne and looked forward to Tom Ferguson's arrival. He had had a very difficult time trying to please Henry and quite honestly would be pleased to see him go.

Tom joined his wife at the Fergusons staying until the Kings moved out, Mrs King having come out from the U.K. to join her husband for their round of farewells. These were many, some thrown by European friends but the most lavish were the

Chinese banquets provided by the various contractors as a tribute to a man who they respected and of course they had depended upon over the years. At these banquets many courses were served, each course being washed down with brandy or whisky *yam sengs* which literally means "bottoms up."

A typical menu might include such dishes as Shark's Fin and Bird's Nest soup, Tiger Prawns (steamed or fried), Chinese Roast Pork, Crab Fu Yung, Sweet and Sour Pork, Peking Duck and many other bewildering delicacies. Their generosity was overwhelming and "face saving" being what it was, often led a contractor to serious debt. Most guests went home to face monumental hangovers on the next day. Because of her condition Sarah was permitted not to attend, the smell of garlic and some of the herbs made her sick.

The McMillans seemed a likeable pair. Tom was a quiet man who went about with an air of pre-occupation which gave quite the wrong impression, he was both shrewd and astute and always impeccably mannered. Like Henry he had been 'in the bag' and as with so many others he bore the scars of internment, not enjoying the best of health. Daphne his wife was the extreme opposite, being both vivacious and outgoing. She dressed in the height of fashion, can-can petticoats being the rage at that time. One was led to believe from her conversation that she loved parties and was in the habit of throwing many. Geoff thought to himself "life is going to improve round here."

If she gave the impression of being frivolous this was short-lived for underneath the facade was a strong-willed woman, as they were about to find out. She too had been interned by the Japanese and her determination that she and her fellow prisoners should survive had caused her to fall foul of the Camp Commandant. When she protested at the appalling shortage of food and had been insistent in her demands he in his anger had drawn his sword across her jaw line causing her to be permanently scarred. She never referred to the years spent as a POW unless asked and her replies were brief. She and Tom were devoted to one another. It was of course a great disappointment that they had no children and partly explained her keen interest in the forthcoming arrival of the Farrers' baby.

Shortly after the Kings departure when the McMillans had settled in they threw a party, and everyone was invited. Daphne had worked wonders with the house in the short time they had been in it: she was without doubt a born home-maker. Dark corners had a new lease of life brought into them by her magnificent floral arrangements, no easy task as so many of the flowers in Malaya whilst thriving in the garden immediately wilted on cutting. The atmosphere was further enhanced by the presence of Gopal, Henry King's house boy, who had been kept on by the McMillans. He loved a party and circulated amongst the guests attending to their drinks also exchanging a few words with those who knew him well. No one was in any doubt that he went with the house. The atmosphere was warm and friendly, and Geoff felt that this was the start of a new era.

The day following the party Sarah was due to go into hospital as the the baby was two weeks overdue. Daphne's driver and car collected both Sarah and Geoff in the afternoon calling in at the manager's bungalow on the way out. They also had Fatimah, their new *amah* with them, it being an ideal opportunity for her to visit her mother and return to the estate later with Geoff.

Daphne was pleased to see them. She was excited at the prospect of the baby's arrival — more so than Sarah, who by now was feeling apprehensive about the experience ahead of her. They checked into the hospital, with Geoff staying for a while until Sarah seemed more relaxed. He left promising to return the next day when hopefully something would be happening. They drove straight back to the estate calling in on Tom and Daphne to let them know that everything was fine and that the doctors would be inducing the birth tomorrow morning.

Driving up to the bungalow Geoff was somewhat surprised not to be met by Gerry who normally came racing out when he heard the cattle grid rattle. Going up the steps he paused at the top, then for some reason did not go directly into the bungalow but walked round to the back. His heart stopped. Gerry was lying on the ground dead, his body twisted and face contorted in pain. Calling the SCs, Geoff dropped on one knee to examine the dog. He thought that it had been shot. Finding no blood or bullet wounds, his next thought was poison — but how?

First on the scene was Ah Choy as the SCs arrived,

"Allah Mat!" cried Kassim.

Geoff told them that he thought Gerry had been poisoned - perhaps he had eaten something,

"Or drunk something," added Ah Choy.

"Good God," thought Geoff. "The water!" only then noticing the fast dripping tap. He immediately sent Kassim up to the police quarters warning the wives not to use the water till it had been checked out. He next phoned Tom who arrived at the bungalow in what seemed like seconds. The dresser was rushed up to the bungalow to test the water. He performed his tests and said that he believed that sodium arsenite[1] was

[1] *Sodium arsenite was extensively used for the eradication of lallang, the destructive grass that was the curse of every rubber estate, and the killing of trees. Because it was so deadly (cattle would die if they ate grass sprayed with it) very strict precautions had to be enforced as regards to storage, accountability and protective clothing. It followed that there was a major enquiry on the estate and the drum was taken away for examination by the police.*

present in the water. The police in Kajang were informed about what had happened and came out to the bungalow bringing a chemist and a vet who confirmed that there was sodium arsenite in the water and that the dog had drunk some and died. An order was given that no water must be used from the supply and a tanker was sent up from the factory as an emergency measure.

"Am I glad that Sarah knows nothing about this!" said Geoff to his manager, who added: "Yes, and I think that we would be best advised not to tell her."

When the police returned to Kajang with the chemist and the vet, the police officer in charge stayed on and together with Geoff and the SCs went down into the jungle-covered re-entrant and traced the water pipe down to the pond which was the source of their water supply. There was a track of sorts. They soon saw the water through the trees and, as they emerged from the undergrowth, the pump. The hydraulic ram was set in concrete and worked continuously, driven by a head of water held in a concrete tank into which water passed through a filter. Lying half submerged in it was a blue and white drum with the words "sodium arsenite" painted on it.

Among the callers at the estate the next day was Mr Timpson from Head Office, Chairman of the company in KL. He like everyone else was worried about what had happened and especially the immediate security of the Farrers. It was decided there and then that Geoff should move as a temporary measure into the Fergusons and his bungalow's water supply should be attended to. The SCs were to remain using water brought by tanker daily. It was recommended that the Farrers take local leave when Sarah was discharged from hospital and that they should stay at the company's beach-side bungalow at Port Dickson. Geoff accepted the idea immediately.

CHAPTER VII

After he had left, Sarah was put through all the necessary examinations. She then settled down to the hospital routine. The induction was to start the following morning and in the meantime she set about getting to know some of the other patients. With the exception of herself they had all had their babies and were only too willing to recount the experience, so time passed quickly.

The following day everything seemed much as normal, and although the induction had taken place nothing seemed to be happening. It wasn't until the evening after Geoff had left, having spent the afternoon with her, that positive signs indicated that the baby was on the way. Nothing was going to happen in a hurry, she was assured by the midwife. As it happened, baby Elaine made her arrival at 3am. She weighed 7lb 13oz, had a fine pair of lungs and masses of dark hair. Sarah felt rather proud of herself and lost no time in telephoning Geoff at the estate who thought that he should come immediately until he was persuaded that mother and daughter should sleep for the remainder of the night. He duly arrived at the hospital at 7am, was delighted with his daughter and stayed a short while. He then had to return to the estate as there was some bother that had to be sorted out in the coolie lines.

Sarah was due to stay in the hospital for ten days. She imagined that the time would drag but this was not so as life was centred round the baby's routine and of course the visitors. She hadn't realised that they had so many friends. After the initial excitement of the baby's arrival she had a bout of homesickness — after all Elaine was a first grandchild for both sets of parents and it seemed strange for them not to be there. Geoff visited every day but would stay for short periods only. He looked worried but in answer to Sarah's questions would make light of things, blaming labour force problems.

On the sixth day after the birth Geoff told Sarah that they would be going to Port Dickson and not the bungalow on the estate when she and the baby came out of hospital. She was bewildered. They had hoped to go there later in the year when the baby was a few months old, so why this sudden haste to go immediately and why had she to stay in hospital for an extra three days when she was perfectly well? Geoff broke the news to her that Gerry was dead, that he'd been poisoned by drinking the water that came into their bungalow and consequently it was not safe for them to return there until the whole system had been de-contaminated. That would take at least two weeks to complete. Sarah was devastated when she thought of Gerry's horrible end and was even more upset as the full implications of the situation registered with her. They might all have been poisoned and died in agony. It was scarcely comprehensible — who would want to do such a thing?

Geoff switched conversation to the merits of the seaside bungalow at Port Dickson and what a wonderful place it was. They would have a fantastic time there, for not only would they take Fatimah with them, there would also be the resident Chinese cook and *amah* provided with the bungalow. As there was plenty of accommodation they could invite friends to stay, making it ideal.

Sarah scarcely heard a word of what he said. Her mind was full of the horror of what had happened and what might have been. All this had taken place whilst she was in hospital content with the baby and her plans for the future. It explained Geoff's short visits, worried looks and the excuses about problems with the labour force.

Eventually they got down to making arrangements. It had been decided that Daphne would accompany them and stay for a few days and for this Sarah was grateful — it would be great to have her company. The amah and two of the SCs were to come along leaving the rest to look after the bungalow.

They left Bungsar Hospital on the Saturday and drove straight to Port Dickson. Their car had been returned to them that week looking almost new. Geoff drove with Sarah, Fatimah and the baby in the back, their two SCs Kassim and Ah Choy followed later with Daphne in her car.

The bungalow was everything that they had dreamed of and they immediately fell in love with it. Situated on the beach surrounded by palm trees, a spacious verandah ran the length of the building looking out to sea with a sun lounge at one end. There were three bedrooms with bathrooms, a large lounge and dining room all of which were comfortably furnished. Everything had worked out much better than Sarah had anticipated and she quickly settled down to enjoy their stay. The Chinese cook and *amah* were excellent and Fatimah took to looking after Sarah's needs and the baby. Daphne stayed three days then reluctantly returned to Ulu Tiram and Tom.

Many friends came to visit including some of Geoff's old comrades from the Malay Regiment Depot, which was just a mile up the road. A curry tiffin on the second Sunday saw not only Tom and Daphne come for the day but also Rob and Catrina Ferguson from Puchong Estate and four other friends. A great day was had by all, swimming in the sea followed by curry tiffin and then resting in the sun lounge. Sarah of course had to take things gently but Fatimah and Daphne saw to that. They went to bed quite early that night because Geoff had to go to Sri Menanti the following day.

On the following morning Geoff set out early for Sri

Menanti. The ancestral seat of the Yang di Pertuan Besar (*Yan Tuan* for short) it was in Negri Sembilan not far from Kuala Pilah. Both he and Sarah had been invited as guests at the ceremony of paying homage to the *Yan Tuan* by forty-seven ruling chiefs of the territories that made up the state. Unfortunately Sarah was unable to come on this occasion but hoped that perhaps she might have another chance in three years' time, for it was a triennial ceremony. Their invitation, which was in itself an honour, came by virtue of Geoff being the Officer Commanding the Volunteers in that state.

Having parked the car he joined the already numerous guests and officials gathering near the imposing Hall of Audience with its dome-shaped covering and hangings of yellow silk and velvet. Travelling on the road that morning the skies had been black as far as the eye could see in all directions and Geoff felt certain that the whole pageant could be rained off, but as he approached Sri Menanti the sky cleared locally and the sun burst through. Geoff thought of the *Pawang* no doubt smiling happily: he had earned his one hundred dollars for that day for ensuring that the spirits provided good weather. *Pawangs* have been performing miracles at a small charge for thousands of years, long before Islam, which of course does not recognise their power, nevertheless they provide a colourful part of Malayan heritage.

While people were waiting for the ceremonies to start the band of The 1st Fiji Infantry Regiment were playing on the lawn, colourful in their scarlet coats and unusual "skirts." There were other attractions across the gardens where men, in pairs, dressed in black *sarongs* and *baju* gave an exhibition of *bersilat*, the Malay art of self-defence. They were unarmed on this occasion but it is sometimes performed using a *kris* (Malay dagger) held in the hand. The movements of the arms and hands were as carefully rehearsed as those of the feet and although the occasional lightning blow was delivered with the open hand(serving as a *kris*), or by foot whenever a vulnerable point was exposed, the greater part of the time was taken up by graceful and stealthy manoeuvring, in time to a gong, a long two-ended drum (*gendang*) and a Malay clarinet (*serunai*) A little way beyond them was a troupe of dancers, the men in line facing a line of girls. The girls sang a *pantun* (a four-line verse of wit and epigram). Each man, taking it in turn, responded to a verse as they too danced to the music of the orchestra made up by a three-string viol played by an elderly man, two or three players strumming about ten single-ended drums with their fingers and hands and another sounding five small inverted gongs placed face upwards on a small wooden frame.

Eventually the guests were summoned to sit on chairs in the hall facing one and other at right angles to the dais, the chiefs and minor chiefs being already in position on the carpeted floor. His Highness and the *Tungku Ampuan* (his wife) then took their seats on the throne to a salute of seventeen guns. In response to the heralds' summons, commencing with the senior chief Pengghulu Luak Ulu Muar, they each in turn carried out the ceremonial. There was a salute with hands raised palm to palm, fingers pointed upwards to touch the bridge of the nose. This was done three times. There then followed a slow sequence of moving the hands to the right down to touch the *kris* and back to the forehead and then back to the waist. This was done seven times each by each chief as he mounted the steps to the throne, each one trying to put more into it than his predecessor. Geoff, although very interested, found himself dropping off from time to time. The heat and the fact that he had helped Sarah feed the baby in the middle of the night had made him rather sleepy.

The drive back to Port Dickson was tortuous and slow as hundreds of guests made their way home. When he finally reached the bungalow Fatimah met him at the door with his silver tankard full of cold Carlesberg. He went into the sun lounge and told Sarah all about the day's events and who was there that they knew. He turned down the offer of tea, changed into his trunks, walked out into the sea and luxuriated in its freshness.

He came back into the sun-lounge as the sun was receding in the West

"Oh!" said Sarah, remembering a phone call she had taken earlier that day. "That chap we saw in Bentong asked if he could call in to see you tomorrow at about eleven. I told him, 'Sure, stop for lunch.'"

Geoff looked at his wife and said: "Who, dear — what chap?"

Sarah got up and walked over to the telephone where she picked up a piece of paper on which she had written the name "John Patch."

"I wonder what he wants?" asked Geoff.

Next morning they went in the sea before a breakfast of *pappaya*, baked crab, coffee and toast. Geoff was expecting Sergeant-Major Hamid to call with some papers for him to sign which he did about 10.30am. Fatimah had brought in some coffee and biscuits and he and Geoff were reminiscing about the days when they served in Pahang, when Hamid stopped, looked directly at him and said: "*Tuan*, I think that Wuh Pun is still alive."

"But that is not possible," argued Geoff. "You have read the papers and seen the reports. He was killed by one of his own people."

Hamid paused and then said: "All that has been happening

to you recently only makes sense if he is still alive."

This made Geoff's blood go cold. He thought for a while, shook himself and said "No, no — it can't possibly be so".

Sensing that perhaps he had spoken out of turn, Hamid got up to go, just as Fatimah came into the room to announce that a *Tuan* Petch was at the door (she had difficulty saying "Patch").

"Come in John, come in," called Geoff. "Meet Inche Hamid, my PSI with the Volunteers. We've been together off and on for four years or more — since he was a corporal, in fact."

They shook hands.

"Hamid has just told me that he thinks that Wuh Pun is still alive and is the cause of my troubles. I told him that it was impossible."

John paused and then said: "I have come to tell you that fingerprints matching those of Liew Kim the terrorist who had killed his two comrades prior to surrendering have been found on the steel drum that contained sodium arsenite. It looks like he's our man. However Hamid's proposition will need to be looked at further. I can tell you that Liew Kim has failed to make his obligatory check in at Seremban for the past three months. I also know that prior to going into the jungle he and his mother and father were illegal immigrants squatting on land south of Triang. That means that we had no way of confirming his claim to be who he claimed to be. His mother died during the war and his father is supposed to have been killed by Malays in a period of racial retribution in 1946.1 must say that Hamid's hunch may well turn out to be true. I will get back to Bentong now and check on Wuh Pun's death and identification."

He shook hands with Geoff and Hamid, shouted his apologies to Sarah, who was feeding Elaine, then drove off.

CHAPTER VIII

Wuh Pun never forgave himself for the killing of Ah Loy. If he hadn't persuaded her, because of her advanced state of pregnancy, to take shelter in the *atap* hut on the edge of that jungle clearing she would still be alive. He had been taking her with him to the meeting that was to be held at Sunget Ruan near Raub where Chin Peng, the Leader of The Communist Party, was expected to make an appearance. Wuh Pun's star was high with the Party and he felt that his presence there would further enhance his prospects of promotion.

As Political Commissar he gave lectures at camps at various jungle locations and ran courses at his own base near Jerkoh. Here they were given lectures on Marx, Lenin, Stalin and Mao Tse-tung and on the successful armed revolutions in China, French Indo-China, Burma and the Philippines. The importance of attacks on rubber estates and tin mines so as to disrupt the Malayan economy was stressed. Communism, he explained, could then take over with public support in the resulting chaos.

When the expected victory did not materialise Wuh Pun began to think more deeply. He noted the excesses of the leaders in taking more of things that were in short supply for themselves rather than share with their comrades and on occasions had seen young girls and women brought into the jungle for their pleasure.

They were being harried constantly by the Malay Regiment patrols, many of their men being killed. He himself had been most fortunate when an officer and three men set out to capture him. They were working on information received and they approached a jungle shelter near Tras and called on him to surrender, not realising that another terrorist was with him. When the two made a dash for it they captured the wrong one.

Surrender leaflets were being dropped in millions from the air and a number of junior comrades had defected. They had been offered safe conduct and a reward, with extra for their weapons. The Leaders said that many were shot by the British, however they made possession of such a leaflet an offence punishable by death. Then came the bombshell, the surrender of Hor Lung the Commander of the so-styled Malayan Peoples Anti-British Army in South Malaya — information on which the Government held back for some time before releasing. Rumours had reached the Party chiefs in Pahang who suppressed it. Wuh Pun was devastated.

He now turned his thoughts towards getting out of this mess. As he believed that the death penalty would be mandatory for him because he had personally murdered two *towkays* in Kuala Lipis shortly after Ah Loy's death, he now hatched the cruel plan which he believed could save his skin.

The plot basically centred on cultivating a friendship with Lim Meng, the District Committee Member whom he despised and would be quite happy to kill, indeed it would be a pleasure. But the most important person would be Liew Kim who was Lim's bodyguard and whom comrades said looked so like Wuh Pun. Liew was the ideal identity to assume as he had no record in Malaya. His parents were illegal immigrants who had slipped into Malaya through Thailand and had squatted on an isolated holding near Triang. His mother had died during the Japanese occupation and his father had been killed by Malays when he wandered into a Malay Reservation in 1946. Liew had only discovered his father's body because after his murder the Malays had buried him in a shallow grave and when 'rigor mortis' set in his arm had stiffened and stuck up out of the ground. All that was required was the opportunity. This came near Bentong and had been so easy.

His two comrades were sleeping soundly when at 5am he stabbed each of them in the heart and he hacked them with his *parang* with a fury that surprised him. He drove himself with such frenzy that he was quite exhausted. He lay there awake waiting for daybreak before hiding the weapons, then walked out through the rubber estate to the main road where he bathed in the river and changed into his spare clothes.

His interrogation by the police had been much easier than expected. They accepted his story and after recovering the hidden arms he felt better. He had to go out a couple more times with the police jungle squad but only managed to lead them to a couple of food dumps and an empty camp. He was then allowed to re-settle in Seremban where he reported daily to the police station. He was paid the money for surrendering which amounted to a large sum, much more than he had ever handled before. Reporting was changed to weekly.

It was after reporting in one week that he called into a café and picked up an English newspaper where he read that the volunteers in Seremban were to have a new Commander, Major G C Farrer, ex-Malay Regiment, who was now a planter at Ulu Tiram Estate near Kajang. Wuh Pun stared at the accompanying photograph.

"That's the bastard!" he exclaimed. "I never thought that I would see him again but the gods have given me a second chance to honour my vow. I will not fail again."

Wuh Pun moved within days to Serdang, a village between the Ulu Tiram Estate and Kuala Lumpur, setting up as a freelance interpreter selling his services to the many semi-illiterate people who required assistance with form filling and so on. Many of these people and their relatives worked on Ulu Tiram

Estate and he was able to build up a picture of the place and make his plans for revenge. The first thing he did was kill a drunken Sikh policeman and steal his sten gun which he hid in oilcloth in a hole in the ground near to the estate.

When he heard of the forthcoming flying fox shoot to celebrate the cessation of emergency regulations in that area, he determined to use it as an opportunity to attack Farrer at his bungalow. Unfortunately his lack of experience in night warfare let him down and he turned his mind to other ways.

One of his clients turned out to be in charge of the spraying team working under contract at Ulu Tiram controlling the elimination of *lallang*. Wuh Pun had learned one skill well as a terrorist and that was how to blackmail people. Despite his desperate pleading the man finally agreed to drop a half-empty drum of sodium arsenite between the weighing shed and the pool rather than have his two sons castrated. When Wuh Pun put the drum and its contents into the intake of the water pump he felt sure that he had extracted his revenge on Farrer and he prematurely celebrated his success in Kuala Lumpur that night.

However the next day he learnt of his failure and saw the man that he had blackmailed taken into custody for questioning. He thought it wise to leave Serdang immediately and move to the anonymity of Kuala Lumpur where he lay low cursing his bad luck, and determined that next time that he took on Farrer it would be face to face and there would be no chance of failure.

CHAPTER IX

There had been hints dropped that the company wanted to move Geoff to an estate near to Karak in Pahang to replace someone who was going on six months' extended leave. Geoff was not happy about it and together with Sarah he managed to get permission to go and visit the place. Geoff had served in Pahang and, realising that things were a bit primitive there, he wanted to check out just what they would be let in for.

His worst fears were correct. The estate was very run-down and the man whom he was to replace was living in squalor with his Chinese mistress in a very sub-standard building next door to the factory. There was no kitchen as such except for an open fire over which hung what could only be described as a cauldron.

One look was enough, so they made a hasty departure back to Selangor. Geoff assured Sarah that nothing on earth would get him to move there with a wife and a newborn baby. He of course had lived in conditions 100 per cent worse in the jungle but what they had just seen was not acceptable for normal life.

On the way back through Kuala Lumpur Sarah reminded Geoff that the General had asked him recently to call in to discuss an idea that was in his mind next time he was in town. This seemed to be a suitable opportunity so they drove into the Ministry of Defence (MINDEF). The General was away, but his deputy, a Brigadier with whom Geoff had also served, told him that he believed that the War Office in UK would look kindly on any request for his re-commissioning and secondment to the Royal Malay Regiment. In view of what they had just seen and believed to be on the cards for them in the world of rubber Geoff had no doubt about what to do. He signed the necessary forms to initiate the process and went to tell Sarah what he had done.

Back on the estate Geoff reported to Tom McMillan on his visit to Pahang making it absolutely clear that he would not move his wife and child into accommodation such as he had seen. Tom agreed but said that nothing was definite yet and that he would tell Head Office about his report. As the cost of any new accommodation would come directly out of the manager's commission he could not see the present incumbent doing anything in a hurry.

For the next week estate life went on as normal but the suspense was getting through to them both. Geoff told Head Office that if the company were to insist on him moving to Pahang he would resign, and as they were entitled to passages home Sarah and Elaine could fly home to UK to stay with her parents and return to Malaya after a week or two. Meanwhile he would stay on and find something else. He hoped that his application to rejoin his Regiment would be successful but did not mention this to them.

The following Saturday they had a long-standing invitation to a party held by the staff of the RRI at the experimental station at Sungel Buloh. The parties there had a reputation of going on all night so Sarah's departmental head who actually lived there wangled it that she could have the use of the old visitors' bungalow, which was currently out of use, on that night.

It was a very attractive bungalow if somewhat old, of wooden construction with an *atap* roof and set in what had once been an orchard of Malayan fruits. In addition to an old durian tree, there were *mangosteen, duku, langsat* and *mata kuching* growing in abundance. Honolulu Creepers grew up the sides of the house and cascades of pink flowers hung down over pergola-like constructions outside the place.

The bedroom was large and airy with a king-sized bed over which hung a huge mosquito net down to the floor. Overhead was a ceiling fan and there were steps down to a concrete floored bathroom of the old Malayan style. It had a flush loo, two Shanghai Jars containing icy cold water and a zinc dipper or ladle with which one had to scoop up the water to take a primitive shower. There was also a wash bowl with running cold water.

When Sarah and Geoff arrived with Elaine and a portable cot her boss had made arrangements for the daughter of his servant to sit in with Elaine while the party was on. She would leave when they returned from the party.

That night they had a great time meeting many old friends but withdrew at about midnight and made their way back to the bungalow. It was very hot and there was little or no breeze. Geoff thanked the babysitter and gave her a couple of dollars as she left. He was soon stripped and ready for bed. He cleaned his teeth andgot under the mosquito net, having switched on the overhead electric fan. As it was so hot he did not put on his *sarong* (standard sleeping dress) but folded it over his stomach to protect himself from getting a chill. Baby Elaine was fast asleep in her cot at the foot of the bed. Sarah always took longer doing those things that a woman has to do and eventually she too climbed in under the mosquito net where Geoff was already asleep. As it was so warm she left the sheet folded back to the foot of the bed and she too fell asleep.

Geoff slept well and was enjoying a dream in which he felt an exploring hand move up his leg. He probably had a broad grin on his face as his own hand moved to welcome the intruder, when suddenly he awoke with a loud yell. There perched on his manhood was a bloody bat! What was more there were bats inside the net, and bats outside the net all greatly disturbed by the fan which was going full speed. The light was still on, adding to their confusion. Sarah woke, dived straight under the mattress and refused to come out. No amount of threats, pleading or drawing her attention to the plight of the baby could get her out. In fact she demanded that he clear the beasts out of the net before she would even take a peep.

He managed to remove the bats that had forced their way into the mosquito net and then to switch off the fan and light.

Eventually when all the creatures had all withdrawn from the room and Geoff had closed the shutters on the windows he got back into bed. He was quite shaken by the whole thing and sought solace in Sarah's arms only to be told: "Get away from me! Go and have a shower. There is no knowing what those bats had on them."

He went down into the bathroom, splashed a bit of water about, making noises to convince Sarah that he had braved the cold waters in the jars, then returned to bed for a warm.

Meanwhile in hiding in KL, Wuh Pun had developed a morbid paranoia the more that he thought about his life and what it might have been if he had not embraced Communism and taken the only person that he had ever loved away from her family to a violent death. His own life no longer mattered to him — there was just one purpose left, the killing of Farrer. He knew that his target went to Seremban each Sunday, now he set about finding a suitable spot to observe the approach of his victim and kill him. He found just the place near Mantin.

He could not retrieve the sten gun that he had buried near Ulu Tiram but had noticed that some planters were in the habit of putting their weapons behind the bar where they drank in Batu Road. It was quite simple for him to steal one and get away before the loss was discovered.

CHAPTER X

It was Sunday and Geoff, if he was honest with himself, knew that he had taken too much on. He was leaving Sarah in the bungalow alone all day while he went off to the Volunteers. Baby Elaine had been awake most of the night and he was glad to be off to a change of environment. He went to early Mass in Kajang where in the tranquillity of the service he reflected on his life and thanked God for his good fortune in having Sarah for his wife and Elaine for his baby daughter. His mind was reflecting on the recent happenings when he became aware that the small congregation was already leaving the church. He quickly got up, left the pew and made his way to his car.

He drove full speed to Seremban, slowing only to pass through the checkpoints at either end of Semenyih New village. When he arrived at the camp the company were already drawn up beside the vehicles waiting on his word to embus. They were off to Port Dickson Ranges to complete their Annual Classification. The journey was uneventful and it was not long before the first detail was firing. The men looked forward to the event and the standards of marksmanship were very high. The scores of two of the corporals, Felix Santa Maria and Punnusamy were worthy of Bisley — of which of course neither of them had ever heard. It was getting late in the afternoon by the time they returned to Seremban and having cleaned and stored their weapons the company dismissed. Geoff now had to get back to the estate, shower and change before going into KL for dinner with an old chum, Ken Pitt, who had just arrived back in Malaya and was breaking his journey to Alor Setar in the North.

Leaving Seremban, Geoff drove like the clappers hoping to

do the journey in record time, and was coming out of a double S-bend when he saw it. There was an overturned motorcycle on the grass verge and a man obviously hurt lying face down on the roadside. He stopped the car and ran over to see what he could do.

"Bloody hell! What the f***'s this?"

As he approached, the man rolled over and fired three rapid shots from a hand gun. Geoff threw himself into the ditch on the other side of the road.

"Walked right into it, you bloody fool," he thought as he quickly pulled his Smith and Wesson .38 from its holster.

He saw his would-be assassin closing in for the kill. He would never forget the look on the man's face. He had never seen such hatred.

They both fired simultaneously and the assassin fell with a grunt. Only then did Geoff realise that he too had been hit. Blood was soaking through his jungle green trousers but strangely he felt no pain.

"Never mind that just now," he told himself as he crawled along the ditch before raising his head. As he did so a shot rang out and a bullet tore through his right shoulder epaulette removing the brass crown with a metallic ping.

"Bloody close that — I must keep my cool and not do anything foolish," he thought. "Someone is bound to come this way soon — there is no need for heroics at the moment."

After what seemed an eternity but was probably just a few minutes, an armoured three-tonner came up through the bends. As it did so a shot rang out. Geoff, who had partly raised himself to wave to the vehicle, dropped down flat but just had time to see four Gurkhas jump out of the vehicle. Three ran to the assassin and the other directly to Geoff with a grin on his face so typical of a Gurkha. He immediately set about applying a field dressing to Geoff's wounded thigh. His three comrades shouted out that the Chinese was dead.

They helped Geoff to his feet and assisted him over to where a body lay slumped on its side. It required no expertise to see that the man had put the muzzle of his weapon into his mouth and fired, blowing the back of his head and brains out.

The Gurkhas were full of laughter and smiles, and while two stayed at the scene Geoff had the driver and the one who applied the dressing drive him in his car to the next police post to report the incident and phone Sarah.

They took Geoff to Kajang Hospital where his wound was cleaned and stitched up. It appeared to be nothing worse than a flesh wound and Geoff was just insisting that he be allowed home when Sarah appeared together with Tom the estate manager.

"What on earth are you two doing here?" asked Geoff, not realising the worry his ambush had caused. The medics gave him an injection of pain killer and tranquilliser and recommended no alcohol for twenty-four hours — advice which was of course ignored. They got back to the bungalow where Sarah got a message to Ken at the Railway Hotel telling him about what had happened.

Geoff was just saying that Sunday evenings were a bit of a bore when the sound of cars driving up to their bungalow alerted them. It was Tom and Daphne together with Ken whom they had secretly contacted and collected. The medics' advice was soon forgotten.

The following day saw a procession of callers at the estate, many of whom were well-wishers that they had never met before. Geoff was beginning to feel quite a celebrity. He spoke to John Patch over the phone who said that he would drive over later in the day to see him and that an SEP (Surrendered

Enemy Personnel) who had served with Wuh Pun and Liew Kim had made a positive identification of the body.

Sarah asked Geoff: "Will this mean that our lives will be a little less hectic from now on?

She might have known better.

Word came through that he was to be given an award by HH The Yang di-Pertuan of Negri Sembilan in whose State Geoff's action had taken place. It would be the state's Meritorious Service Medal, the PJK. Later in the day Mr Timpson from Head Office called together with Tom McMillan and it was amicably resolved that the couple would not go to Pahang, that Geoff could resign his appointment in a month's time, so as to qualify for his annual bonus and that the company would pay for their passages home. This was altered so that just Sarah and Elaine would take a return flight as and when they wanted it. This suited the Farrers fine and no doubt the company too, but everything had been done in a most friendly manner and friendship continued with the McMillans thereafter.

A message came from the General that he wanted to see Geoff and Sarah on the Wednesday afternoon at Headquarters. There he confirmed that Geoff was to receive his majority in the Regiment in three months' time when he was to move to Kedah in north Malaya to lead a Special Task Force in operations on the Thai Border against a large Communist force operating from the Betong Salient.

GLOSSARY

I have used the phonetic system of romanised spelling in use in Malaya at the time.

Tuan - Master, Lord, used to persons of position e.g Haji or a ruling prince (and always to European men prior to the late 1960s).

Dia perempuan, Tuan, dia belum mati - It's a woman, she's not (yet) dead.

Gelap tidor - Dark (go to) sleep.

Ada - The verb to be. In this case meaning yes.

Nanti sini - Wait here.

Suda - Adverb. Past; completed. Can also mean yes.

Suda kenyang? Are you satisfied? i.e. Have you had enough?

Terimah kaseh - Thank you.

Atap - Roofing thatch of palm leaves.

Mem - Europan lady.

Amah - Maid servant.

Songkok - A Malay man's velvet cap.

Kebun - A garden (*tukang kebun* = gardener).

Stengah - *Sa-tengah*, a half.

Parang - A chopping knife, a machete.

Keretah sudah lari - The vehicle has "run off".

Lopong (Chinese) - Stupid fellow.

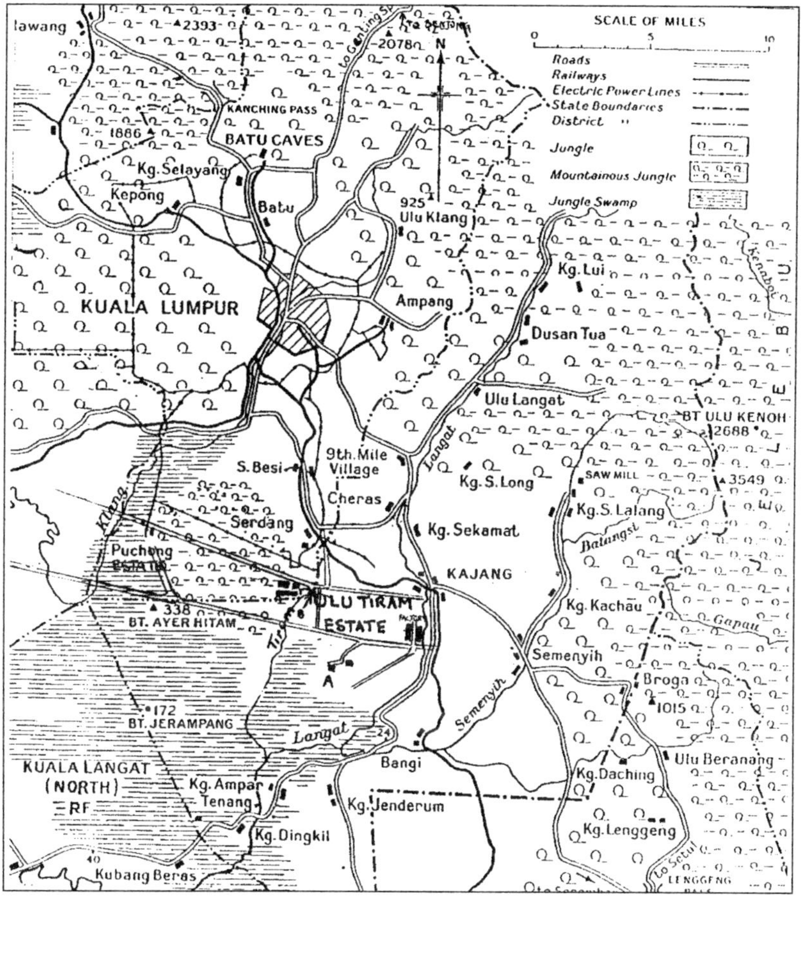
SCALE OF MILES
0
5
10
Roads
Railways
Electric Power Lines
State Boundaries
District
Jungle
Mountainous Jungle
Jungle Swamp
N
Rawang
2393
2078
KANCHING PASS
1886
BATU CAVES
Kg. Selayang
Kepong
Batu
925
Ulu Klang
KUALA LUMPUR
Ampang
Kg. Lui
Dusan Tua
Ulu Langat
BT ULU KENOH
2688
3549
SAW MILL
Langat
Kg. S. Long
9th. Mile Village
S. Besi
Cheras
Serdang
Kg. S. Lalang
Batangsi
Kg. Sekamat
Klang
Puchong ESTATE
KAJANG
Kg. Kachau
Gapau
338
BT. AYER HITAM
ULU TIRAM ESTATE
FACTORY
A
Semenyih
Broga
1015
172
BT. JERAMPANG
Langat
24
Bangi
Ulu Beranang
KUALA LANGAT (NORTH) RF
Kg. Ampar Tenang
Kg. Jenderum
Kg. Daching
Kg. Lenggeng
Kg. Dingkil
40
Kubang Beras
LENGGENG